BAZ LUHRMANN

ICONS OF CINEMA

First published in the UK in 2024 by Studio Press,
an imprint of Bonnier Books UK,
4th Floor, Victoria House, Bloomsbury Square, London
WC1B 4DA
Owned by Bonnier Books, Sveavägen 56, Stockholm, Sweden

www.bonnierbooks.co.uk

Copyright © Emily Maskell, 2024

1 3 5 7 9 10 8 6 4 2

All rights reserved.
ISBN 978-1-80078-986-9

Written by Emily Maskell
Edited by Stephanie Milton
Designed by Maddox Philpot
Production by Hannah Cartwright

This book is unofficial and unauthorised and is not endorsed by or affiliated with Baz Luhrmann.

A CIP catalogue record for this book is available from the British Library

Printed and bound in China

The publisher would like to thank the following for supplying photos for this book: Alamy and Getty. Every effort has been made to obtain permission to reproduce copyright material but there may be cases where we have not been able to trace a copyright holder. The publisher will be happy to correct any omission in future printings.

EMILY MASKELL

UNOFFICIAL AND UNAUTHORISED

Contents

The Curtain Rises...	**6**
The Showman	6
Luhrmann's Cinematic Universe	8
What Makes a Luhrmann Film?	12
Australia's Auteur	14
The Red Curtain Trilogy	16
Strictly Ballroom	**18**
A Cinematic Debut	18
A Familiar Story	20
Breaking the Mould	24
Paso Doble Flare	30
The Last Dance	34
William Shakespeare's Romeo + Juliet	**38**
An Unsentimental Shakespearean Adaptation	38
DiCaprio and Danes	42
Fated Lovers	46
Religious Iconography	50
A Criminal Romance	56
Moulin Rouge!	**62**
The Red Curtain Trilogy Conclusion	62
A Tragic Musical	66
Theatrical Theatre	76
'El Tango de Roxanne'	80
'Elephant Love Medley'	84
Australia	**88**
An Adventure Epic	88
Over the Rainbow	94
Stars Down Under	96
The Real History	102
Luhrmann's Outback	106
The Great Gatsby	**108**
Literary Adaptation	108
The Myth of Man	114
The Roaring Twenties	118
A Weekend at Gatsby's	122
Under the Eyes of God	126
Elvis	**130**
The King of Rock 'n' Roll	130
Remodelling the Biopic	134
Elvis on the Mic	136
Blues and Gospel	142
Las Vegas Tragedy	146
The Curtain Falls...	**150**
In Another World	152
Luhrmann's Cinema	154

THE CURTAIN RISES...

The Showman

Over three decades, Mark Anthony Luhrmann, who goes by the moniker Baz Luhrmann, has cemented himself as one of cinema's most recognisable filmmakers. The Australian film director, producer, writer and actor has worked across television, opera, theatre and music, but it is in the cinematic realm where he has really flourished. He is regarded as a contemporary auteur renowned for his theatrical aptitude, opulent aesthetic and sweeping romances.

Luhrmann is a showman as much as a director, known for conducting dramatic narratives that play out on a flamboyantly grand scale. Culturally, his significance spans the arts as he takes classic narrative structures and morphs them through new perspectives, not limiting himself to the boundaries of realism. This signature style marks the Australian filmmaker as a pioneering storyteller where the fusion of high and low pop culture creates an entirely singular body of films.

OPPOSITE: Luhrmann on the set of *Moulin Rouge!*

Luhrmann's Cinematic Universe

A chronological voyage through Luhrmann's cinematic works begins with his directorial debut, *Strictly Ballroom* (1992). The romantic comedy charting a dancer rebelling against tradition oozes with Luhrmann's love of ballroom dance.

Then came Luhrmann's sophomore feature, *William Shakespeare's Romeo + Juliet* (1996). His interpretation of Shakespeare's famous play modernised the tragedy but retained its Shakespearean English. The romantic spectacle showcased Luhrmann's ability to give an already well-known story a new lease of life.

In the early 2000s, Luhrmann released *Moulin Rouge!* (2001), one of his greatest masterpieces. The jukebox musical romantic drama is a sonic pastiche packed with eclectic pop culture references that Luhrmann grounds in a transfixing romance.

OPPOSITE TOP: Luhrmann on the set of *Strictly Ballroom*.

OPPOSITE BOTTOM: Luhrmann on the set of *Romeo + Juliet*.

BELOW: Luhrmann directing Nicole Kidman on the set of *Moulin Rouge!*

ABOVE: Luhrmann on the set of *Australia*.

OPPOSITE TOP: Luhrmann on the set of *The Great Gatsby*.

OPPOSITE BOTTOM: Luhrmann on the set of *Elvis*.

Australia (2008) saw the director venture into particularly ambitious epic territory. Set between 1939 and 1942, this dramatised character study channels grand epics of old for a love story set in northern Australia against a backdrop of World War II.

The Great Gatsby (2013), an adaptation of F. Scott Fitzgerald's 1925 novel of the same name, took Luhrmann's love of adorned excess to new heights. The glitz and glamour of the 1920s upper class becomes a playground for the director to explore.

Nearly a decade after *The Great Gatsby* comes *Elvis* (2022). Dealing with larger-than-life characters is not new for Luhrmann, but chronicling the King of Rock 'n' Roll's career is a mammoth task he thoroughly commits to.

What Makes a Luhrmann Film?

Luhrmann's filmography is an array of quirky stories united by their existence as beautiful tragedies. Infatuated with fated romances between star-crossed lovers, the director is unapologetically brazen regarding heightened emotions.

Luhrmann is known for his instantly recognisable signature style – characteristics we'll refer to as 'Luhrmannisms' throughout this book. A theatrical and glamorous aesthetic of excess has become synonymous with the director. He designs cinematic spectacles to inspire wonder; the costumes are extravagant, the editing is swift, the soundtracks are catchy, and the scale of the films is wondrously grand.

However, he is also a cinematic provocateur. Pulling back the curtain on his approach to filmmaking, Luhrmann deliberately exposes and exaggerates artificiality. He invites audiences to step into his sensory-stimulating cinematic worlds that embrace the sublime, the ridiculous and the romantic with open arms.

ABOVE: Luhrmann directing on the set of *The Great Gatsby*.

LEFT: Luhrmann on the set of *Moulin Rouge!*

Australia's Auteur

Born in Sydney, New South Wales, in 1962, Luhrmann's Australian identity is central to his work as a filmmaker. Not only does Luhrmann return to Australia for several films, but his cinematic motifs are firmly embedded in Australia's cultural psyche.

Luhrmann is one of Australia's most commercially successful directors. Four of his films are in the top ten worldwide-grossing Australian films: *Australia* is at number two, *Moulin Rouge!* at number six, *The Great Gatsby* at number seven and *Elvis* at number nine. Also, the director's oeuvre is lauded internationally; his films have garnered an impressive four Academy Awards, four Golden Globes and 12 BAFTAs.

Other than *Strictly Ballroom* (on which he was not a producer), Luhrmann has served as writer, director and producer on every film he has made, overseeing the assorted elements of costume, soundtrack and production design. Additionally, with his wife Catherine Martin, Luhrmann created his production company Bazmark in 1997, which spans films, TV, fashion and advertising.

ABOVE: Luhrmann and Catherine Martin at the 2002 *Vanity Fair* Oscar Party.

OPPOSITE: Luhrmann and Kidman at the 54th Directors Guild Awards.

The Red Curtain Trilogy

"The show will be a magnificent, opulent, tremendous, stupendous, gargantuan bedazzlement," says Harold Zidler (Jim Broadbent), the owner of the Moulin Rouge in Luhrmann's 2001 film. Though he is describing a musical within the film, Zidler's sentiment is true of Luhrmann's entire Red Curtain Trilogy.

Luhrmann himself grouped his first three features and gave them the Red Curtain label to define the elevated style that unites them. There is no plot connection between the three movies. Instead, it is the commitment to intense theatrics that links the trio. In *Strictly Ballroom*, emotion is communicated through dance; the poetry of language is central to the lovers of *Romeo + Juliet*; and in *Moulin Rouge!* the nature of theatrical performance is at the film's core.

The films comprising the Red Curtain Trilogy share distinct characteristics – they each reveal the film's ending in the opening moments, and they are all set in a heightened world – but above all else, these films feel more connected to the world of theatre than to that of filmmaking. Built around amplified entertainment, this story trilogy is intended to enthral and amuse with engrossing stagecraft transformed for the screen.

OPPOSITE: Scott (Paul Mercurio) and Fran (Tara Morice) in *Strictly Ballroom*.

ABOVE: Juliet (Claire Danes) and Romeo (Leonardo DiCaprio) are in love.

LEFT: The dramatic cabaret in *Moulin Rouge!*

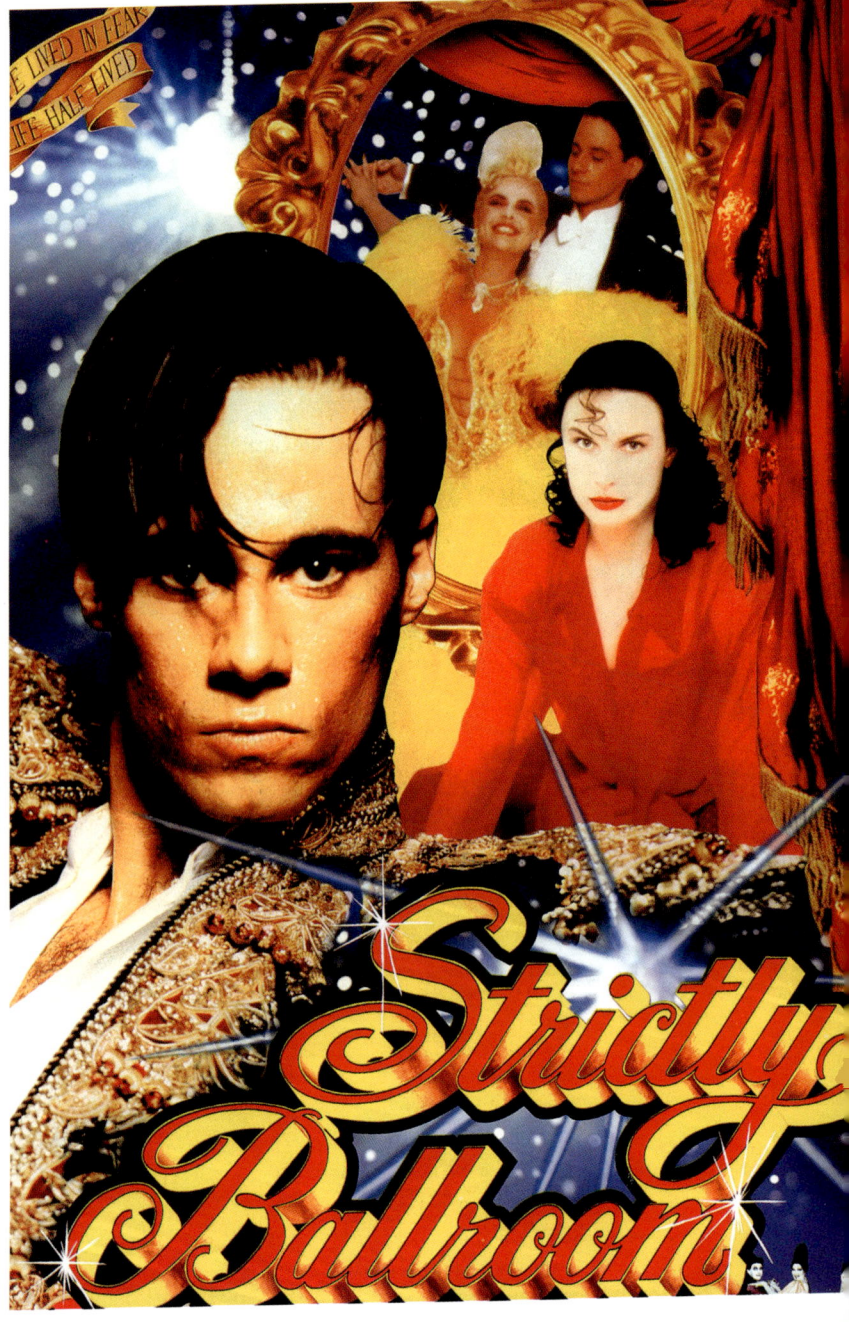

STRICTLY BALLROOM

A Cinematic Debut

The year was 1992 when Luhrmann burst into the world of cinema with his feature debut, *Strictly Ballroom*. The Australian romantic comedy is a love story and a love letter to the cutthroat world of competitive ballroom dance. *Strictly Ballroom*'s infectious energy, theatrical storyline and bold, metaphorical visuals foreground Luhrmann's instantaneously striking signature style.

Strictly Ballroom originated as a short stage play devised by Luhrmann and fellow students in 1984 during his studies at Sydney's National Institute of Dramatic Arts. Alongside Craig Pearce, Luhrmann expanded the comedy-drama script, adding more developed thematics to the underdog narrative for the 1986 Czechoslovakian Youth Drama Festival.

The story goes that during the play's run at Sydney's Wharf Theatre in 1988, music executives who would go on to found M&A Productions became enchanted by Luhrmann's vision. M&A Productions approached Luhrmann to adapt his play for the screen. He agreed – on the condition that he would direct. Australian writer Andrew Bovell was brought on board to translate Luhrmann's story

OPPOSITE: The *Strictly Ballroom* poster.

ABOVE: Luhrmann and the *Strictly Ballroom* cast at the film's premiere.

from stage to screen. Also, Pearce reinstated his co-writer credit to channel the play's theatrical grounding.

Luhrmann's ambitious first Red Curtain Trilogy film faced hardships in production, with a slim AUD three million budget. The production team had to get crafty with money-saving options, including shooting performances in a real competition at Melbourne's Sports and Entertainment Centre. Despite these workarounds, *Strictly Ballroom*'s flashy blend of romance and comedy charmed audiences and collected an impressive AUD 80 million at the worldwide box office, making it one of the most successful Australian films ever.

ABOVE: Ballroom dancers (Leonie Page, Gia Carides, Sonia Kruger).

OPPOSITE TOP: Two young dancers (Lauren Hewett and Steve Grace).

OPPOSITE BOTTOM: Liz (Carides) and Scott (Mercurio) dressed ready for the competition..

A Familiar Story

When it comes to their debut film, a director's choice of story is always revealing, and *Strictly Ballroom* holds a quietly poignant familiarity for Luhrmann. The film is loosely inspired by the director's youth studying ballroom dance as a child. Like *Strictly Ballroom*'s protagonist, Scott Hastings (Paul Mercurio), Luhrmann's mother was a ballroom dance teacher. Though the characters aren't exact copies of people from Luhrmann's life, there is an undeniable connection underscoring *Strictly Ballroom*.

The film was also partly inspired by the life of the late Keith Bain, a pioneer of modern Australian dance as an Australian Ballroom Exhibition Champion and Latin-American Champion. Though his entry into competitive ballroom dance entertained the crowd, his inventive and untraditional style bewildered the judges. *Strictly Ballroom* implants Bain's isolating experience of professional ballroom rejection into Scott's character.

Luhrmann's film provides an immediately intense welcome to the glitzy but garish world of

ballroom dance as viewers chassé onto the dance floor alongside the competitors of the Southern Districts Waratah Championships. Mid-routine, Scott commits a ballroom cardinal sin and breaks out "his own flashy, crowd-pleasing steps" consisting of unchoreographed, wild spins and floor slides that disgust the judges as well as his dance partner, Liz Holt (Gia Carides). Luhrmann's lens, though, is in awe of such movements; extreme slow motion narrows attention to Scott's unexpected execution.

Scott returns to Kendall's School of Dance – where his mother, Shirley (Pat Thomson), and her long-time dance partner, Les Kendall (Peter Whitford), coach up-and-coming talent – to be reprimanded for his non-federation floor craft. He struggles to deal with a furious mother, the loss of his dance partner, and the judgement of the Ballroom Confederation's chagrin hanging over him. Here, Luhrmann demonstrates that the medium of dance is a form of dialogue. While Scott and Les argue about the approaching Pan Pacific Ballroom Championship, the two men tango. It's a dance of confrontation which fosters a stealthy but majorly dramatic attitude. Luhrmann amps up the scene's intensity with swift shots that move alongside the pair's staccato movements, keeping up with their pace as rebellion confronts tradition.

The meeting of Scott and Fran (Tara Morice), a young Spanish-Australian "beginner", also sees dance choreography become a dialogue. Enthralled by Scott's unorthodox moves, Fran pitches herself as his dance partner. The scene becomes a visual poem: they dance the rhumba ("the dance of love") to the instrumental opening of Cyndi Lauper's 'Time After Time' under dramatic chiaroscuro lighting. They hold intense eye contact as their torsos move close, and wobbly first steps develop into a synced rhythm. Cinematographer Steve Mason's camera dances with them as Luhrmann foreshadows romance in movement, not words.

RIGHT: Fran (Morice) ready to dance the paso doble.

OPPOSITE: Fran (Morice) holds Scott (Mercurio) in a dip.

Breaking the Mould

Luhrmann has never been a filmmaker who abides by convention nor simplifies his stories to a singular genre identifier; *Strictly Ballroom* is neither a romance, a drama, or a musical but intertwines conventions of all three. On the surface, the film is a love story between

ballroom dancers. But look deeper: you will uncover an allegory of individual revolt and a commentary on the indispensability of artistic expression.

Both Scott and Luhrmann are mavericks who sidestep tradition. Luhrmann's film centres on the fallout of stifled self-expression. "I'm sick of dancing somebody else's steps all of the time," Scott proclaims, frustrated by the uncompromising and rigorous rules. *Strictly Ballroom* also departs from expectation with its boisterous sense of comedy. From characters falling on freshly mopped floors to some intentionally bad wigs, the breaks from the competitive plot see Luhrmann bring a sense of playfulness to his direction. Humour is epitomised in the iconic scene where Liz pleads for their rival, Ken (John Hannan), to enter and declare: "Pam Short's broken both her legs, and I want to dance with you." Her wish comes true. Mere seconds after her plea, this exact event then plays out.

LEFT: Fellow competitors Ken (Hannan) and Liz (Carides).

For all its embedded rebellion, *Strictly Ballroom* does see Luhrmann contrasting Scott's novel moves with traditional aspects of the ballroom dance. The rhumba is an integral marker for Scott and Fran's budding romance, and backstage at the State Championships, the pair quietly dance the steps. For Luhrmann, it's a hugely stripped-back scene as Scott realises it's not winning he desires, but Fran. Luhrmann frames their passionate but unshowy dance against a red curtain backdrop in a two-shot that smoothly moves with their steps. It's a significantly different presentation than the bold make-up and high hairdos on the other side of the curtain.

Relying on the rhumba's slow but sensual movement, Luhrmann's implication of brewing infatuation is clear; Scott and Fran's connection isn't limited to the dance floor. Luhrmann shoots Scott's confession to Fran with a chain link fence separating viewers and the lovers. However, when they lean in to kiss, the camera moves beyond the chain link barrier; it's a visual metaphor of the wall between acting and reality crumbling as the dancers take their romance off the dance floor.

Alongside Luhrmann's two protagonists, Scott's discreet father, Doug (Barry Otto), has a significant subplot surrounding unconventional choreography. During an evening rehearsal, Scott and Fran hear someone in the building, so they flee to the rooftop. Luhrmann initially follows them before panning down the building's exterior and re-entering the dance studio through a window to see a man emerge from the shadows. It's Doug. The stiff, unassuming middle-aged man steps into the spotlight and suddenly bursts into dance, wild moves which share a likeness with his son's steps.

OPPOSITE: Fran (Morice) and Scott (Mercurio) ready to dance the paso doble.

It's not until just before the Pan Pacific Ballroom Championships that Scott discovers his father's love affair with dance. Les breaks the news to him – that Doug was "potentially the greatest ballroom dancer this country has ever seen" – in an attempt to warn Scott against following in his father's footsteps. Luhrmann zooms in on an image of Doug and Shirley dancing, transporting viewers back to 1967 when the couple were ballroom champions. But Doug's enamoration with improvised dance leads the federation to expel him. He is so heartbroken he vows to never return to the dance floor. A theatre play illustrates this narrative from the past – it's not only a meta nod to *Strictly Ballroom*'s origin but a reinforcement of the layers of showmanship performativity within Luhrmann's film.

OPPOSITE: The contrasting male figures in Scott's (Mercurio) life include Doug (Barry Otto), Barry (Bill Hunter) and Les (Peter Whitford).

BELOW: Scott's father, Doug (Otto), went rogue with his different ballroom steps.

Paso Doble Flare

Though Scott and Fran perform several ballroom dances throughout *Strictly Ballroom*, their rule-breaking paso doble is the most memorable. The Latin ballroom dance imitates a bullfight; the male dancer is the matador, while the female dancer is the red cape of a toreador. After another heated argument with his mother, Scott arrives at Fran's home and confesses his desire to dance with her at the competition. However, Fran's Spanish family does not warmly receive his declaration. Fran's father, Rico (Antonio Vargas, one of the world's leading Flamenco dancers), is especially suspicious of the young man and demands to see his paso doble in action.

They gather on the wooden terrace, lit by lanterns with Fran's family playing live instruments, as Scott and Fran's dance is met by taunting laughter. Rico can't just stand by and watch; he assumes the matador position, head held high with steely confidence and effortless finesse. The family form a ring in which Rico challenges Scott with a "this is how it's done" glare. They look like two bullfighters facing off. Luhrmann holds an extreme close-up on the ferocity of Rico's footwork, while the sound design focuses on the increasingly loud clicking of his heels. Rapid-fire editing cuts jump between close-ups of Rico's dancing and Scott's wonderment. The fiery

moment melts into a scene of schooling between the two men, who are very different from one another.

Rico becomes Scott and Fran's unofficial dance coach to help them perfect their paso doble. Fran's grandmother Ya Ya (Armonia Benedito) also assists: she hits Scott's chest to engrain the rhythm of the music into his soul to help him "dance from the heart". Their nightly rehearsals are brought forward into the daylight, no longer hiding in the dark – it's a subtle callback to Fran's sentiment that "a life lived in fear is a life half lived". Luhrmann characterises such scenes with a naturalistic soundtrack composed of the nearby railway station's rhythmic rattling, the family's clapping and the hammering of mops.

OPPOSITE TOP: Fran (Morice) and Rico (Vargas) dance together.

OPPOSITE BOTTOM: Scott (Mercurio) rehearsing at Fran's (Morice) family home.

ABOVE: Scott (Mercurio) and Rico (Vargas) rehearse the paso doble.

Meaning is not only conveyed via their movement but also through their garments. Ya Ya stitches Fran's homemade dress skirt, the flowing vermillion fabric accentuating her steps. Despite the restraints of a limited budget, the glamorous Flamenco-inspired dress that Fran goes on to wear at the championships is visually triumphant, with its heavy jewelled ruffles and elaborate layers.

Fran's look directly contrasts with ballroom costume designer Angus Strathie's kitsch creations that externalise the inner workings of absurdly satirical characters. The federation costumes provide a superficial veneer – neon blue eyeliner, fake tan and ostrich feathers – which is perfect for the dance floor but a stark contrast against Fran's homemade, meaningful dress. Scott's bejewelled matador jacket is also a noteworthy look. The golden, glittering costume is like a suit of armour donned to go into his final battle; Scott exudes heroism as he rises to the challenge of confronting the federation's perspective.

OPPOSITE: Ya Ya (Benedito) admiring the dress she made for Fran (Morice).

RIGHT MIDDLE: Costume designer Catherine Martin with *Strictly Ballroom* performance costumes.

RIGHT BOTTOM: *Strictly Ballroom* costumes on display.

The Last Dance

In *Strictly Ballroom*'s final moments, Luhrmann revisits notions of dance as a medium of expression. Scott freezes mid-argument with his mother as his father's voice rings out around the Pan Pacific Ballroom Championship arena: "It was the dancing that mattered… we lived our lives in fear." To this point, Mercurio's performance sees

ABOVE: Rico (Vargas) and Ya Ya (Benedito) clap for Scott (Mercurio) and Fran's (Morice) final dance.

OPPOSITE: Fran (Morice) and Scott (Mercurio) take to the dance floor.

Scott torn between head and heart. But this scene sees the young man soften with Fran's advice – "a life lived in fear is a life half lived" – finally making sense.

As Federation President Barry Fife (Bill Hunter) spouts that he's been rigging competitions, Scott knee-slides onto the dance floor to disrupt proceedings. Luhrmann's vibrant direction reaches its apex; under the brightest spotlight, the director holds close-ups of his determined dancers, the camera moves in line with their

ABOVE: Fran (Morice) and Scott (Mercurio) defy the federation judges.

choreography while whooshing sound effects punctuate their spins. As expected, the federation judges disqualify them. But Fran and Scott refuse to leave the dance floor; the camera flies across the room to see them stare at the judges with the same steely confidence that Rico once faced them. A singular clap pierces through the crowd's stunned silence. It's Doug. He is creating a rhythm for them to continue dancing. For a moment, the world goes silent. Scott's racing heartbeat is the only audible noise as *Strictly Ballroom*'s hero decides his next move: he raises his arms in a display of mutiny and begins to dance. Luhrmann shoots an extreme close-up of Scott's footwork; the roles become reversed as Rico reacts with amazement. The music resumes as Luhrmann's camera becomes Scott and Fran's third dance partner, gliding along with their perfectly executed movements, concluding with Fran's final spin as Scott rises from a knee-slide to meet her. It's a euphoric moment as the crowd goes wild and descends onto the dance floor.

Luhrmann's film leaves the question of whether Scott and Fran won the championship unanswered. Moreso, it's irrelevant. *Strictly Ballroom* concludes with a hero shot of Scott and Fran's kiss, a consummation of their romance perfectly timed to the swell of John Paul Young's delirious disco gem 'Love Is In The Air'. Luhrmann regards their rebellion on the dance floor as a trophy. As his camera pulls back, the dancers get swallowed by the swarming crowd. With its effervescent energy and theatrical flair, *Strictly Ballroom* is a perfect introduction to Luhrmann's increasingly evocative filmography.

WILLIAM SHAKESPEARE'S ROMEO + JULIET

An Unsentimental Shakespearean Adaptation

Luhrmann lifted the sonnets of William Shakespeare's doomed romance *Romeo and Juliet* for his capacious sophomore feature. He grasped at the opportunity to go bigger and bolder following the unexpected success of *Strictly Ballroom*. With *Romeo + Juliet*, Luhrmann intended to imagine how Shakespeare would interpret his play if he were a director while making the Shakespearean world accessible to the "MTV generation". Modernising the 1597 story of two teenagers, Juliet Capulet (Claire Danes) and Romeo Montague (Leonardo DiCaprio), the director inserts countless Luhrmannisms into this timeless tale of star-crossed lovers.

Abiding by the Red Curtain Trilogy formula, Luhrmann quickly establishes the film's relationship with the source text. Utilising Shakespearean prose and playfully capturing the rhythm of Shakespeare's iambic pentameter, *Romeo + Juliet* sees some of the playwright's most quotable lines delivered in new and imaginative ways. For instance, the famous prologue – "Two households, both alike in dignity, in fair Verona, where we lay our scene" – is spoken by a news reporter explaining the ongoing conflict between the feuding

OPPOSITE: The *Romeo + Juliet* poster.

families of the House of Montague and the House of Capulet. Then, Luhrmann slams through the TV screen into a quick-fire montage of Mexico City and Veracruz, reimagining Shakespeare's Verona.

Luhrmann modernises without preciousness. For instance, he draws this story into contemporary life by swapping swords for guns, but retaining original references with pistol names like dagger and rapier. His brashly imaginative version of the play also reinterprets the feuding families as violently competitive business empires. An establishing shot of the city sees two opposing skyscrapers branded with each family name. Family representatives standing at opposite ends of Luhrmann's frame, while police discipline them over civil unrest, reinforces this visual division.

Another notable change is the diversity of characters. Though Shakespeare's play features extensively white characters, Luhrmann reinterpreted these identities for his film's casting. Take Romeo's best friend, Mercutio (Harold Perrineau); Luhrmann reimagines him as a Black, queer man who is the life and soul of the party. Mercutio arrives at Romeo's side, blasting Kym Mazelle's version of Candi Staton's 'Young Hearts Run Free'. With a diamante halter neck crop top and short shorts paired with a bright white wig, Mercutio's character is the perfect bridge between Shakespeare's dramatic writing and Luhrmann's modern theatrics.

There's also the charismatic Tybalt Capulet (John Leguizamo) with his seductively villainous entrance. Soundtracked by the fizzle of a match, the Latino man steps out at a petrol station to confront the hotheaded de facto Montague gang. With slicked-back hair and wearing a red vest branded with the Virgin Mary, Tybalt's expression sours as he spits his distaste for the word "peace". The tumultuous Tybalt is a character that Luhrmann utilises as an instigator of violence, with his pure and unwavering hatred for the Montagues, specifically Romeo. Leguizamo and choreographer John O'Connell elevated the showy character of Tybalt by designing his movement during gunfights to look like a flamenco-inspired dance – stylish but deadly.

OPPOSITE: Rival families: The House of Capulet and the House of Montague.

ABOVE LEFT: Mercuito's (Perrineau) performance at the Capulet mansion.

ABOVE RIGHT: Rival families: The introduction of Tybalt (Leguizamo).

DiCaprio and Danes

DiCaprio's Romeo and Danes' Juliet portray a seraphic side to the otherwise dark and troubled families. The actors' beguiling chemistry exudes the smitten innocence and besotted desperation of an all-consuming young love. Their youthful exuberance is so entrancing it is easy to forget about the tragic fate that lies ahead.

In *Romeo + Juliet*, DiCaprio's role demonstrates and advances his nineties heartthrob status. Luhrmann sets up the first look at Romeo with budding anticipation. He is perched on Verona Beach's Sycamore Grove theatre, shot from a distance and silhouetted by the hazy light of an absurdly stunning golden-hour sunset.

A slow-motion pan up Romeo's body imitates the gaze of a lingering admirer, taking in the star's sharp jawline, cherubic face and mischievous grin. Luhrmann reveals Romeo like a pin-up, with his half-unbuttoned suit and cigarette dangling from his lips as floppy blonde curtain bangs droop over his eyes. Radiohead's moody track 'Talk Show Host' soundtracks the moment, the teasing lyrics

bolstering the desire that DiCaprio summons: if you want me, come and find me – I'm waiting. He lifts his gaze directly to the camera, holding eye contact, daring viewers to tear their attention away from his alluring charm.

OPPOSITE: DiCaprio behind the scenes with Luhrmann.

ABOVE: Romeo (DiCaprio) at golden hour.

LEFT: DiCaprio and Danes behind the scenes of *Romeo + Juliet*.

ABOVE: Juliet (Danes) stares at Romeo (DiCaprio) with wide-eyed infatuation.

LEFT: Juliet (Danes) with angel wings on her balcony.

OPPOSITE: Luhrmann and Danes behind the scenes.

Juliet's cinematic introduction is also an otherworldly moment. Viewers meet Juliet as she is submerged in the bath, holding herself underwater with her eyes wide open, experiencing a rare moment of silence in the Capulet household. She resurfaces and hurries to her mother (Diane Venora), who dresses her for the family's costume ball. Stepping onto her famous balcony, draped in a pure white dress paired with angel wings, Juliet admires the colourful fireworks overhead that also reflect on her dewy skin. This singular shot sees the meeting of Danes' projection of ethereal innocence alongside Luhrmann's beautiful framing that renders the shot like a wistful painting.

Though Danes imbues the hopeful ingénue with a shy softness, there's no sacrifice of sharp awareness. The character vehemently rejects requests to marry eligible bachelor Dave Paris (Paul Rudd), even though he would be the answer to her family's woes. It is Romeo she craves, with her blush-dusted cheeks and wide-eyed infatuation. Under Luhrmann's direction, Danes carves a singular effigy of Juliet that honours but updates the original.

Fated Lovers

The Capulets' abundant costume ball is the exquisite location for the love-at-first-sight meeting of Romeo and Juliet. An uninvited, party-crashing Romeo is taking a break from the madness of the evening in a bathroom when he becomes entranced by a tropical aquarium filled with colourful, shimmering fish. Amongst the tank's coral, he spots a coy eye staring back at him. It belongs to Juliet. The scene is amongst the film's most pastiched moments as the lovers, dressed as an angel and a knight, chase each other's gaze like inquisitive fish on opposite sides of the tank. Luhrmann cuts back and forth between their silent infatuation as their surprise turns to glimpses of interest, before evolving into longing stares.

From the Capulets' grand hall, a performance of Des'ree's 'I'm Kissing You' articulates Romeo and Juliet's sudden swell of emotion. With no dialogue, Romeo and Juliet's eyes catch with the lyrics "the aching". It's a subtle connection but a pinpointed note of yearning commanded by Luhrmann's frequent collaborator, editor Jill Bilcock.

Driven by a newfound lust, the pair stumble into a lift to share their first kiss. Luhrmann captures their giddy excitement with spinning camera movement and soaring strings that come crashing down with the realisation that they belong to opposing houses. Juliet is positioned at the top of the staircase, looking down at Romeo, who is gazing up at her – the blocking inspired by the famous balcony scene – for the revelation. Their physical standing also mirrors their positionality: Juliet is expected to marry a favourable bachelor with

TOP LEFT: Juliet (Danes) through the fish tank.

TOP RIGHT: Romeo (DiCaprio) through the fish tank.

MIDDLE: Romeo (DiCaprio) and Juliet (Danes) meet at the fish tank.

BOTTOM: Juliet (Danes) and Romeo (DiCaprio) can't take their eyes off each other.

upward mobility, while Romeo is a wayward young man untamed by familial expectations.

Depicting one of Shakespeare's most iconic scenes, Luhrmann alters the placement of Juliet's balcony monologue after Romeo has scaled the wall to see her. In Luhrmann's visual interpolation, he swaps the original balcony blocking for a swimming pool. It is a daring change, allowing Danes and DiCaprio to inject their interpretations of their characters' chemistry.

Though Luhrmann makes heavy cuts to Shakespeare's written dialogue, the scene dispenses the same meaning through visual metaphor. After Romeo spooks Juliet and they tumble into the pool, a nonexistent current draws them together that surges with Romeo's proposal. The scene is taut with sexual potency as their soaked bodies move closer, clothes clinging to their skin and floating hair framing their longing expressions.

Situating the proposal in the Capulets' swimming pool is another instance of Luhrmann using water as a motif for scenes of heightened romance, like the aquarium meet cute. Water submerges Romeo and Juliet in their own private world, and when Luhrmann captures them underwater, the clear pool mirrors their romance's emotional transparency and virtue. In another callback to the aquarium, the same song, 'I'm Kissing You' by Des'ree, plays. It is a rekindling of emotions that sparked by the fish tank but became an inextinguishable flame in the pool.

TOP: Romeo (DiCaprio) is hiding from Juliet (Danes).

MIDDLE: Juliet (Danes) and Romeo (DiCaprio) kiss.

BOTTOM: Romeo (DiCaprio) and Juliet (Danes) float closely in the pool.

Religious Iconography

Another recurring motif throughout Luhrmann's *Romeo + Juliet* is religious iconography. Catholic metaphors and symbolism are rife throughout this tragedy; angelic symbolism is particularly prominent in Juliet's bedroom. As she awaits Romeo, Juliet surveys her collection of winged angel statues – noticeably similar to the costume she wore in her first chance encounter with Romeo. With the soft, golden glow of candlelight on her face, Luhrmann uses notions of angelic purity to oppose Juliet's heady desire for Romeo.

ABOVE: Juliet (Danes) is waiting for Romeo (DiCaprio).

OPPOSITE TOP RIGHT: Juliet (Danes) at candlelight with angel statues.

OPPOSITE BOTTOM: Juliet (Danes) holds a vial of poison.

Catherine Martin's production design and Brigitte Broch's set decoration come into their own in one of *Romeo + Juliet*'s conclusive scenes. An exiled Romeo returns to Verona Beach at the news of Juliet's death, promising: "Juliet, I will lie with thee tonight." Tragically, Romeo has missed the note from Father Laurence (Pete Postlethwaite) telling him Juliet has taken poison to fake her death and that she will rise in 24 hours so the lovers can run away together.

Remaining unaware of Juliet's faux poisoning, Romeo purchases himself some real poison to take his life and join Juliet in death. After being chased through Verona by the authorities, he arrives at the holy edifice, and is greeted by a mesmerising display. Luhrmann reveals the Capulet family's subterranean tomb with an expansive panoramic, ceiling-to-floor shot. Concentrated religiosity is breathtaking in this production design: hundreds of pillar candles blanket the floor with a luminous warmth, neon blue crosses glow brightly in the aisle and Juliet lies motionless on a tomb draped with white sheets as adorned angels look down at her.

ABOVE: Juliet (Danes) is in a bed surrounded by candles.

Luhrmann tracks Romeo's slow approach towards Juliet's lifeless form and unveils his reaction to seeing Juliet before viewers see her. DiCaprio shoulders an all-consuming, raw grief with a tactile touch and a gentle kiss; the once rebellious teen is now a broken-hearted lover saturated by anguish. "Here will I set up my everlasting rest," he declares as he wipes his tears and lies beside her body. Luhrmann conducts the scene with a calmness, even using slow motion, to soothe the film's giddy pacing and prompt an amplified intensity as Romeo prepares for his suicide.

ABOVE: Romeo (DiCaprio) arrives at Juliet's (Danes) side.

As Romeo's lips touch the vial, Juliet's eyes flutter open. It's a moment the viewer is anticipating, yet Luhrmann has brought such individuality to this story that there remains a sliver of hope that Romeo may be saved. Witnessing Romeo's suicide, Juliet's fate is

ABOVE: Romeo (DiCaprio) and Juliet (Danes) on their deathbed.

RIGHT: Juliet (Danes) cries over a deceased Romeo (DiCaprio).

ABOVE: The bodies of Romeo (DiCaprio) and Juliet (Danes) lie still.

sealed. She tries to kiss poison from his lips but to no avail, so she raises Romeo's gun to her temple. She gazes up as if in prayer before she pulls the trigger and falls beside Romeo's body.

Luhrmann's camera comes to a rest with the image of the lovers in an eternal embrace before the aerial shot gradually rises, as if following their souls departing from their bodies. The elevated angle reveals the sheer scale of burning candles that Luhrmann regards with a rare, untampered silence; it's a distinct contrast to the chaos of police lights and sirens that have erupted outside. This tragic ending concludes Luhrmann's portrait of pure heartache. Shakespeare puts it best: "For never was a story of more woe than this of Juliet and her Romeo."

A Criminal Romance

Though *Romeo + Juliet* is rooted in a deep romanticism, the film also straddles a raging criminality with the paradoxes between violence and peace, strife and unity, and sacred and profane. Crime and vengeance underscore *Romeo + Juliet*'s most formidable scenes. The de facto gangs – the crude Montagues and the city cowboy Capulets – repeatedly face off in violent confrontations.

One such scene occurs on Venice Beach as the opposing households clash with deadly force. Romeo arrives with his heart teeming with love – having just married Juliet in a secret ceremony – but his sunny disposition contradicts the brewing storm in the sweltering day's heat.

An angsty Mercutio grows irritated at Tybalt and pulls Romeo's weapon to defend them. However, Tybalt rejects Romeo's desire to forge peace between the households in a kinetic scene of cinema vérité stylings that Bilcock edits with overwhelming ferocity. But Mercutio intervenes and puts his body between Tybalt's glass dagger and Romeo. Luhrmann's mobile camera is thrust in the middle of the altercation. Mercutio stumbles around the beach theatre, an apt location for these amplified dramatics. Furthermore, the pathetic fallacy of thunder rumbling, the wind picking up, and dark clouds rolling in externalises Romeo's devastated rage. The storm, perfectly emulating the scene's tone, was a real-life hurricane that hit the Gulf of Mexico and destroyed some of Luhrmann's sets.

TOP LEFT: The Montague boys.

RIGHT: Mercutio (Perrineau) pulling out Romeo's gun.

BOTTOM: A storm rolls into Venice Beach.

The storm rages on as Mercutio curses both households in his dying moments. Romeo bundles Mercutio's body into his arms, his white shirt soaked with vermillion blood as the hot day turns dark. Luhrmann holds the wide shot for an extended period as Romeo runs the length of the beach to take off after Tybalt while Mercutio's lifeless body lies foregrounded in the sun. This dynamic sequence sees Romeo go from giddy in love to ferocious with grief.

Bloodthirsty for revenge, Romeo gives chase and crashes into Tybalt's car. The latter crawls from the wreck while Romeo stalks him, both men with blood cascading down their faces. Begging to die to be with Mercutio, Romeo holds Tybalt's gun against his forehead. But Tybalt ends up tumbling back, and Romeo raises the gun at him and pulls the trigger.

OPPOSITE: Romeo (DiCaprio) vows to kill Tybalt (Leguizamo).

ABOVE: Romeo (DiCaprio) holds Tybalt's (Leguizamo) gun to his head.

A 21-year-old DiCaprio nailed the character's complicated breadth of reactions, cycling through all of those emotions in a few seconds. His anger is tangible in his animalistic gaze and taunting expression as he fires the gun, but then comes silence. Luhrmann cuts to an extreme close-up of Romeo's expression, DiCaprio's face the only thing visible in the frame. Romeo softens into regret as tears spill from bloodshot eyes and blood trickles down his cheeks. There is no soundtrack for Romeo's breakdown, just the patter of falling rain as he screams: "I am fortune's fool!"

Luhrmann jumps so quickly between the tranquil love and agitated violence that there is no character left untouched by the threat of death. The murders of both Mercutio and Tybalt demonstrate that this burning desire to defeat the enemy household is all in vain. Through Tybalt killing Mercutio and Romeo killing Tybalt, Romeo has not only lost his best friend but left a devastating mark on the households' rivalry. The self-destruction of youth culminates with *Romeo + Juliet*'s heartbreaking conclusion as the two lovers tragically take their lives in each other's arms.

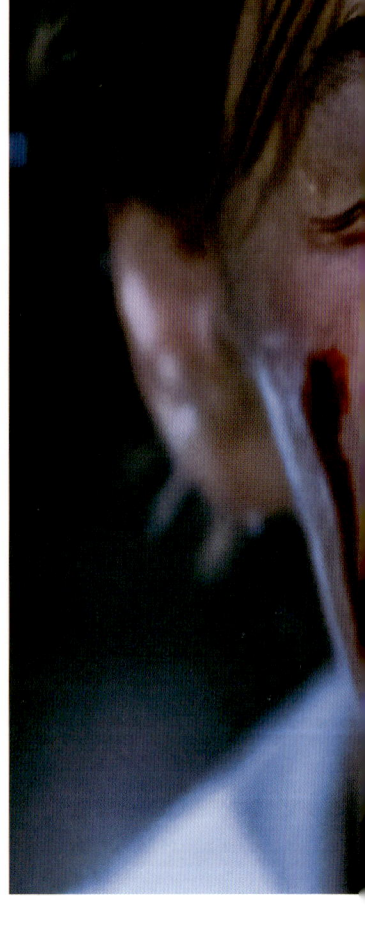

ABOVE: Romeo (DiCaprio) realises he has murdered Tybalt.

MOULIN ROUGE!

The Red Curtain Trilogy Conclusion

Moulin Rouge! is the dramatic finale of Luhrmann's Red Curtain Trilogy. The engrossing jukebox musical romantic drama is a marvel bursting with modern music recontextualised for cabaret, lively dance numbers, and an exquisite explosion of irradiant colour. It is an apt finale to the trilogy – the sweeping romance of a cabaret courtesan, Satine (Nicole Kidman), and a penniless bohemian writer, Christian (Ewan McGregor), proves as wondrously theatrical as it is emotionally devastating. Although the post-modern masterpiece marked the end of Luhrmann's Red Curtain Trilogy, the film heralded a new era for the filmmaker.

Moulin Rouge! arrived after a cinematic musical drought in the 1990s. Luhrmann has shared that he was captured by the desire to reinvigorate the cinematic musical, despite many Hollywood names advising him that the musical would never be popular again in cinema. Luhrmann, however, wholeheartedly commits to the ridiculousness and invites viewers to invest in the fundamental Bohemian ideals: truth, beauty, freedom and love.

OPPOSITE: The *Moulin Rouge!* poster.

ABOVE: Satine (Kidman) and Christian (McGregor) are *Moulin Rouge!*'s lovers.

From the beginning, *Moulin Rouge!*'s elaborate framing structure introduces a meta-narrative where Luhrmann layers a frame within a frame, heightening the mythic foundation of this love story. The film opens by positioning the viewer as an audience member in a theatre. The conductor rises from the orchestra pit, and the red curtain is pulled back to reveal *Moulin Rouge!*'s opening titles. Luhrmann invites viewers into the film through the stage, solidifying that *Moulin Rouge!* exists in the overlap of film and theatre.

Luhrmann's beautifully heartbreaking film predominantly takes place in the iconic Moulin Rouge, the birthplace of the modern can-can dance. Set at the foot of the Montmartre district of Paris, the Moulin Rouge cabaret, a stage for theatrical stories of love and loss, proves the perfect setting for Luhrmann's love story between a writer and a courtesan to unravel. Though the location has become a tourist hot spot, Luhrmann turns back the clock to see the cabaret in its prime.

The film also has an aesthetic typical of the Red Curtain Trilogy. Take the film's introduction to the Moulin Rouge theatre: Luhrmann tracks Christian as he enters the cabaret for the first time, in awe of the spectacle of the Diamond Dogs troupe's energetic choreography. Luhrmann's camera is from Christian's perspective as it navigates the whirlwind of song and dance. The courtesan's bright skirts, kicking legs, and violent spins create a montage of striking imagery that is an overwhelmingly bold welcome into this world.

TOP LEFT: The *Moulin Rouge!* cabaret troupe.

ABOVE: Luhrmann on set with the *Moulin Rouge!* cast.

LEFT: *Moulin Rouge!*'s courtesan cabaret troupe.

A Tragic Musical

Moulin Rouge! begins by revealing its ending. "The woman I love is dead," a dishevelled Christian whispers, sitting at his typewriter as tears fall down his pale face. Christian (who moved to Paris for the

Bohemian lifestyle) and Satine (the aforementioned "woman") are dreamers. They are united in the hope that their love will whisk them away from the shackles of their current lives, but Luhrmann has already established from its inception that this is a tragedy.

Moulin Rouge! is Christian's retelling of his love story with Satine. Within the framework of this narrative, Christian writes the bohemian musical "Spectacular Spectacular" that details the future he hopes to have with Satine. Luhrmann makes these layers of constructed reality malleable; the musical-within-the-film is under constant flux, with characters editing the story to manipulate or mirror what transpires in reality.

OPPOSITE: Christian (McGregor) after Satine's (Kidman) death.

TOP: Satine (Kidman) faces a deadly fate.

RIGHT: Satine (Kidman) and Christian (McGregor) lean in to kiss.

The biggest advocate for "Spectacular Spectacular" edits is the Duke of Monroth (Richard Roxburgh), the financier of the Moulin Rouge who pays handsomely for Satine's attention. Naturally, he is Christian's antagonist. "Spectacular Spectacular" follows a courtesan falling in love with a penniless sitar player (read: Satine and Christian) that she mistook for a maharajah (read: the Duke).

ABOVE: *Moulin Rouge!*'s 'Come What May' musical number.

As the musical-within-a-film's rehearsals get underway, Luhrmann juxtaposes the musical's events with the film's happenings, creating a parallel culminating in a majestic finale. Christian's idealised ending sees romance win as Satine chooses the sitar player instead of the maharajah. But, of course, Luhrmann's film has a more devastatingly heartbreaking conclusion.

ABOVE: Satine (Kidman) performing for the male patrons at the Moulin Rouge.

Death is foreshadowed in *Moulin Rouge!* from the moment Satine appears on a trapeze surrounded by a waterfall of glitter. She is the only person who can silence the raucous Moulin Rouge crowd. Satine flounces onto the dance floor, sparkling in a crystal-embellished mini dress with a matching top hat while performing 'Diamonds Are a Girl's Best Friend'.

ABOVE: Satine (Kidman) is lowered from the rafters into the Moulin Rouge.

OPPOSITE: The Moulin Rouge Bohemians with Satine (Kidman) and Zidler (Jim Broadbent).

Satine returns to the trapeze for her big finale, where a lung-rattling cough erupts from her rouge-stained lips. She manages one shaky inhale before she falls from a worrying height into the arms of a dancer. As Christian puts it: "A force darker than jealousy and stronger than love had begun to take hold of Satine." Such poetic tragedy established so early leaves no room for hope, yet Luhrmann's film will have you wishing that love will conquer all, up until *Moulin Rouge!*'s closing number.

The Moulin Rouge exists in a contained universe. In all its seedy glory, the French fin de siècle setting is an underworld with its own set of rules or lack thereof. Luhrmann frames the power of seduction in the cabaret as crucial for Satine, who will sleep with the Duke to secure financing for the club to become a legitimate theatre. As she prepares to meet the Duke, she rattles off several seduction options to Zidler: "Wilted flower? Bright and bubbly? Or smouldering temptress?" They settle on the latter, knowing that successfully seducing the Duke is Satine's key to escaping the cabaret world and pursuing her acting dream.

From glitzy to seductive, costumes are a conduit through which Satine can claim power. Costume designers Catherine Martin and Angus Strathie set out to create historically accurate looks but with a modern edge in late 19th-century textures and colours. These costumes serve different purposes. For instance, the feather boa-adorned dress exaggerates Satine's moves, while the black lace against her pale skin contrasts the seductive, rouge velvet bed she lies on to seduce Christian.

OPPOSITE: Satine (Kidman) seduces Christian (McGregor).

LEFT: Kidman behind the scenes in a feathered dress.

TOP LEFT: Concept sketch for Satine's (Kidman) diamond dress.

TOP RIGHT: Concept sketch for Satine's (Kidman) red dress.

OPPOSITE: Concept sketch for Satine's (Kidman) feathered dress.

ABOVE: Satine (Kidman) on the Moulin Rouge Elephant's red velvet bed.

ABOVE: Luhrmann directing Kidman on the set of *Moulin Rouge!*.

Theatrical Theatre

The influence of pop culture on *Moulin Rouge!* is extensive. Luhrmann's vaudevillian film not only takes existing music for characters to perform as dialogue, but the director draws on several other sources for his storytelling and visuals. One inspiration is the ancient Orphean myth. Christian is Orpheus, a wildly enchanting musician who descends into a dark underworld to rescue his dead lover. Orpheus is so close to rescuing Eurydice (Satine), but by turning around to see if she's following him, Orpheus sentences Eurydice to death. Luhrmann mirrors the harrowing fate of these lovers as Christian writes his perfect ending with Satine only for their celebration of love in "Spectacular Spectacular's" 'Come What May' finale to be cruelly cut short by Satine's doomed death.

Luhrmann has also noted that Bollywood cinema was a prominent stylistic influence on his filmmaking. Luhrmann was introduced to Bollywood cinema in India while conducting research ahead of directing Giacomo Puccini's opera *La bohème* in 1993. The genre's oscillation between heightened emotional tragedy, playful comedy, and characters spontaneously breaking out into humongous show tunes directly inspired *Moulin Rouge!*.

Similar to Bollywood masala films (films that blend genres like action, comedy and romance), *Moulin Rouge!* borrows from several genres, creating a viewing experience that includes familiarity but remains thrilling. This sense of audience participation, where the flitting emotional register embeds viewers in the film's happenings, is typical of Luhrmann's cinema, which grows progressively grander and louder.

With *Moulin Rouge!* Luhrmann also takes a playful approach and his wicked sense of humour underscores the theatrics. From the ridiculousness of the songwriting process to the Duke's outright ignorance of Satine and Christian's obvious romance, the film jumps between this buoyant comedy and the darker thematics. In doing so, Luhrmann requires a fully invested audience, as his narratives need the viewer's suspension of belief. This notion references early forms of filmic entertainment where black-and-white films required viewers to ignore that they were watching a staged reality so the fictional world could temporarily become their truth. *Moulin Rouge!* is pure in its identity in Luhrmann's cinematic universe with its outrageous characters and far-fetched narrative threads that must be accepted to be understood.

BELOW: Satine (Kidman) in a dance number from "Spectacular Spectacular".

'El Tango de Roxanne'

Moulin Rouge!'s theatrical grounding sets the scene for characters to emote internal thoughts with spontaneous song and dance. Musical breaks appear during Luhrmann's most climactic moments. Take 'El Tango de Roxanne', a ferocious, sexually charged scene that exposes the dichotomy of Christian's jealousy and the Duke's fight for control.

The imperative moment features a large-scale choreographed tango. It begins with a Narcoleptic Argentinian (Jacek Koman), who is part of Christian's "Spectacular Spectacular" company, explaining the dance is about a young man and a sex worker falling in love. The parallel between Christian and Satine is obvious, but the Argentinian is hinting towards his torrid romance with a Moulin Rouge dancer.

The dance chronicles a couple's deteriorating relationship as the Argentinian and his mistress circle each other with simmering desire. Their moves speed up until they execute curt spins and erratic flourishes. "Suspicion!" the Argentinian proclaims, clutching her wrists while she looks towards other men. Toe to toe, he spins them both before marching her backwards, Luhrmann's camera hastily following, spitting: "Jealousy, anger, betrayal!"

The tango, a dance associated with violence and illicit sex, allows Luhrmann to say so much with just choreography. The sequence is one of the most memorable moments for the sheer force of Bilcock's editing, which is as integral to *Moulin Rouge!* as Luhrmann's direction. Bilcock blazes through

PREVIOUS: Satine (Kidman) fears the Duke (Roxburgh).

BELOW: Satine (Kidman) at the Gothic tower.

the sequence – a cut every two seconds escalates the pace to a breathtaking degree. The rapid editing orchestrates a mélange of sporadic camera angles, from shallow focus close-ups to an aerial wide shot where Christian strides through the middle of the dance troupe.

Christian takes the lead now, his jealousy germinating with the knowledge that Satine will spend the night with the Duke. He walks beneath the Gothic tower where his lover stands with another man. In tandem, the explosive, aggressive physicality of the tango mirrors the Duke's surging anger as he spots Satine gazing down at Christian. With Bilcock's kinetic editing moving at a breakneck pace and cinematographer Donald McAlpine's anamorphic lens, it becomes a challenge to identify whether the grasping hands and stomping feet are taking place in the Moulin Rouge or Gothic tower as the dance continues and the Duke assaults Satine. The sharp, high-pitched squeals of violins accentuate the purposefully frenzied scene as the dancer's dizzying spins alternate with the Duke ripping Satine's clothes. In this merging of scenes between the separate locations, Luhrmann depicts the demonic nature of the Duke's jealousy and anger without an explicit scene of Satine's assault.

ABOVE: Satine (Kidman) and the Duke (Roxburgh) in the Gothic tower.

'Elephant Love Medley'

The 'Elephant Love Medley' scene is revered in Luhrmann's filmography. The deeply romantic moment highlights the director's infatuation with sweeping romances and emphasises how he implements soundtrack and lyricism into storytelling. *Moulin Rouge!*'s cacophonous soundtrack is an aural pastiche that transcends genre and juxtaposes typical assumptions of lyrics. Some of the songs in *Moulin Rouge!* have eclipsed their original context through Luhrmann's cinematic placement.

In a confrontation between the bohemian and inamorata, Christian is desperate for Satine to give his love a chance as they ascend the Moulin Rouge Elephant's spiral staircase. As they do so, they sing the 'Elephant Love Medley': an accumulation of love songs from Whitney Houston, David Bowie, The Beatles, Elton John, and many more. Luhrmann employs these lyrics to spell out the push and pull of Satine and Christian's argument as they spar on the Elephant's rooftop. A spellbound Christian begins singing while Satine initially resists his proposal, replying to his melodic voice with blunt speech. Luhrmann shoots the musical moment like a conversation, framing these characters in separate over-the-shoulder shots to reinforce the back-and-forth transpiring through melodies.

Christian then jumps on the Elephant's head, belting his feelings. Satine coaxes him down and then joins Christian in singing, her true feelings coming out as she lets her heart sing. The Moulin Rouge's diamond has learnt to put on a show, but this all melts away as she radiates pure love to Christian with a tender smile and high notes. Her singing partner, too, sets his emotions ablaze as he pours his feelings into the lyrics. The number whisks the pair away from the Moulin Rouge's boisterousness and grants them a world of their own. The songs embedded in 'Elephant Love Medley' span decades and genres, so it's more than likely that any viewer of *Moulin Rouge!* will recognise at least one of these tunes, and the familiarity would hook

ABOVE: Christian (McGregor) on the Moulin Rouge Elephant.

them in. With this soundtrack and dialogue merging technique, Luhrmann gives the impression this story of lovers has existed beyond his film as if it is a fable passed down through generations.

The 'Elephant Love Medley' concludes with Luhrmann's camera spinning around the singing lovers as they commit to each other with a kiss. Fireworks then explode from the heart-shaped walls as the room morphs into a glittering night sky. Though 'Come What May' is a vow between Christian and Satine, 'Elephant Love Medley' is a spellbinding confession of love.

However, the realisation that this scene is from Christian's mourning leaves the moment's sheer romanticism devastating. Cutting between a heartbroken Christian's blue-toned grief and the red-accented highlights of the Moulin Rouge, the divide between tears and laughter seems to broaden with every second.

The 'Elephant Love Medley' scene presents a microcosm of

Moulin Rouge!'s opulent visual style. A culmination of Luhrmannisms across filming coverage, lighting, performances, and colour motifs render the moment a distinct scene of sweeping romance for Christian and Satine's relationship and Luhrmann's filmography.

BELOW: Satine (Kidman) and Christian (McGregor) sing a duet on the Moulin Rouge Elephant.

AUSTRALIA

OPPOSITE: The *Australia* poster.

BELOW: Kidman, Luhrmann, and Hugh Jackman on set.

An Adventure Epic

Luhrmann embarks on his longest film to date: an action-packed 165 minutes, with the adventure epic *Australia*. In a departure from the Red Curtain Trilogy, the director swaps his fascination with musicals for the cultural history of Australia at the dawn of World War II.

This film offered Luhrmann the chance to fulfil the desire to show his homeland in a new light and interrogate the country's relationship with its indigenous population. The director is a self-professed lover of the epic and was keen to bring Luhmrannisms to the genre while balancing elements of romance, war drama and a historical treatise of First Nations people in Northern Australia.

Australia chronicles the converging lives of English aristocrat Lady Sarah Ashley (Nicole Kidman), a hardened cattle rancher named Drover (Hugh Jackman), and Nullah (Brandon Walters), an ambitious 11-year-old Aboriginal boy, between 1939 and 1942. Each embarks on a personal journey of identity and evolution of self. This tale begins when Lady Sarah arrives at her philandering husband's financially failing Australian cattle station, Faraway Downs, to find him dead. Now the sole heir to the land, she is desperate to sell the property and return to her well-to-do life in Britain.

However, Drover scuppers her myopic plan. Luhrmann introduces the rugged Drover in a gradual pan that reveals an untamed beard and sweaty skin before he lunges into a bar fight. Drover and Lady Sarah have a rather hostile greeting – he uses her suitcases to attack townsfolk, resulting in her underwear exploding everywhere – but they find mutual respect as they agree to work together to herd 1,500 cattle for hundreds of miles to secure station-saving fortunes.

Every cinematic epic needs a despicable villain. The Machiavellian Neil (David Wenham) is precisely that in Luhrmann's *Australia*. Neil's introduction demonstrates his heinous cruelty as a sweeping camera shot sees him tying a live fly to a fishing line. He is Lady Sarah's ex-station manager, but is promptly fired when Nullah exposes his plot to take Faraway Downs and create a cattle monopoly with the beef tycoon 'King' Carney (Bryan Brown). He informs Lady Sarah that the men have been stealing the best of her unmarked cattle onto Carney's land for a lucrative army contract to supply beef to the troops.

OPPOSITE: Drover (Jackman) mid-fight.

LEFT: Drover's (Jackman) hero shot.

Nullah is *Australia*'s omnipresent narrator who contextualises each chapter with voice-over while constantly on the run from the police (who want to capture him and send him to Mission Island with other mixed-race children) and Neil (his biological father who wants him dead). Nullah is the film's young hero, and his "magic" grandfather, King George (David Gulpilil), a numinous Aboriginal shaman, is also a valorous character. King George is framed for the murder of Lady Sarah's husband and has fled to a nearby mountaintop from where he observes everything.

With this collection of heroic characters and the film's sweeping scope as a large-scale spectacle, *Australia* is an epic. The amenable genre film wrestles with the tragedy of the 'Stolen Generations' of Aboriginal Australians, clashing perspectives of Aboriginal earthly knowledge and white greed for land and Australian identity facing foreign invasion.

BELOW: Nullah (Walters) peering through Lady Sarah's (Kidman) ranch fence.

Over the Rainbow

Though *Australia* sees Luhrmann move away from the Red Curtain Trilogy, the film still possesses a thread of theatricality. The presence of fantastical, musical eclecticism exists visually with glossy technicolour motifs referencing *The Wizard of Oz*. Trying to soothe Nullah after the horrific death of his mother, Lady Sarah sings a haphazardly memorised version of 'Over the Rainbow'. Kansas is like Northern Australia, an isolated location with tornadoes, dreamers, and adorable pet dogs. Even the name Faraway Downs is a nod to Dorothy's search for a peaceful place that she assumes is "far, far away".

Additionally, although *Australia*'s characters do not skip down the Yellow Brick Road in their antipodean Oz, they embody the mysticism of Kansas's residence. Lady Sarah is the scarecrow, a farmer trying to fit in. Drover is the Tin Man, a mechanical figure who realises the importance of having a heart. Nullah is Dorothy, the dreamer searching for a home, while King George is the Wizard of Oz, a guiding light for these characters.

OPPOSITE: Lady Sarah (Kidman) and Nullah (Walters).

LEFT: Characters from The Wizard of Oz (Judy Garland as Dorothy, Bert Lahr as the Cowardly Lion, Jack Haley as the Tin Man, and Ray Bolger as The Scarecrow.)

In a full circle moment, Nullah watches Victor Fleming's 1939 *The Wizard of Oz* in an open-air cinema, enchanted by Judy Garland's Dorothy. In the pivotal scene where Dorothy clicks her sparkling red shoes, chanting: "There's no place like home", Luhrmann cuts to Lady Sarah and Drover arriving back at Faraway Downs. The editing cut by editors Dody Dorn and Michael McCusker implies that Faraway Downs has become a sanctuary for Nullah. There is also the reality that, like Dorothy, he must eventually leave for his own good.

Stars Down Under

Reuniting with Kidman, Luhrmann forges a very different role for her than Satine in *Moulin Rouge!*. While the courtesan is in her element at the cabaret, Lady Sarah is out of her depth at Faraway Downs. She is the voice of an outsider attempting to find belonging in the wilderness, and her evolution changes with her relationship with the land and people. Though one local remarks to Lady Sarah that "a delicate English rose withers in the Outback," she plants roots in Australia's hardened soil.

Kidman executes the slow but noticeable evolution of Lady Sarah. She arrives at Faraway Downs as a taut, icy and ostentatious woman who learns to thaw under the Australian sun. Her evolution is also apparent in costume, thanks to designer Catherine Martin, who received a Best Costume Design Academy Award for her work. Arriving in the outback, Lady Sarah dresses in crisp whites and elegant tartan blazers fit for dressage. Her refined go-to look may work for afternoon tea in England, but in the dust and the heat of the Australian Outback she sticks out like a sore thumb.

ABOVE: Lady Sarah (Kidman) in her fancy tailored clothes.

OPPOSITE TOP: Lady Sarah (Kidman) is now appropriately dressed for cattle ranching.

OPPOSITE MIDDLE: Luhrmann and Kidman behind the scenes of *Australia*.

OPPOSITE BOTTOM: Lady Sarah (Kidman) and Drover (Jackman) on horseback.

One particularly memorable look is Lady Sarah's dress for the Government House ball. The Asian-inspired red chrysanthemum-printed Chinese cheongsam is a centrepiece of the film's costume offerings. Beneath glowing lanterns, the dress is instantly striking with its elegant high-neck but exposed chest.

Though Lady Sarah's dress is showstopping, the crowd of the bustling ball is reduced to stunned silence when Drover arrives. He is freshly shaven in a full suit and pristine white blazer, worlds away from his usual muddied workwear. For *Australia*, Catherine Martin dug through archival newspapers and interviewed livestock handlers to get an accurate idea of the garments of the time.

Luhrmann also heavily invests in the romance between Lady Sarah and the Drover. Their initial aggressive meeting precedes a humorously uncomfortable night around the campfire. Lady Sarah retires to the camp's only tent but pokes her head out to catch Drover pouring water over his bare torso in slow motion. Luhrmann is not subtle in the ogling of Jackman's muscular male form, but neither is Lady Sarah's wide-eyed gaze.

OPPOSITE: Drover (Jackman) is suited for the Government House ball.

TOP: Lady Sarah's (Kidman) dressed for the Government House ball.

BOTTOM: Lady Sarah (Kidman) and Drover (Jackman) pose in the Outback.

Luhrmann frames their romance like an oasis in the Australian Outback. When they kiss after the Government House ball, their first outing together, the rain pours and thunder claps overhead as locals dance around them with beer bottles held to the sky. The dusty terrain where nothing can grow is given a new lease of life with the downpour, and Luhrmann connects this reawakening of the land with the beginning of Lady Sarah and Drover's confirmed romance.

The connection between land and this romantic partnership is also apparent in Luhrmann's stunning shot composition when the dark outline of a tree against a sunset transitions into the silhouette of

the two lovers kissing. Their love has become embedded into Faraway Downs, as necessary as the water that falls from the sky and the cattle that graze in the pastures.

OPPOSITE: Lady Sarah (Kidman) and Drover (Jackman) kiss in the rain.

TOP: Lady Sarah (Kidman) and Drover (Jackman) kiss in the rain.

ABOVE: Lady Sarah (Kidman) and Driver's (Jackman) silhouetted kiss.

The Real History

With his fourth film, Luhrmann ventures into the realm of historical adaptation. The Red Curtain Trilogy narratives exist in capsule, theatrical worlds of grandeur. *Australia*, however, is more sprawling in its story, which tackles cultural history and socio-political nuances. The second half of the film shifts gears from a Western romance to a war drama as Luhrmann depicts the Imperial Japanese Navy's bombing of Darwin, a city of just over 2,000, which left 197 dead and more than 400 injured.

RIGHT: Drover (Jackman) and Lady Sarah (Kidman) hug at their reunion.

BELOW: Lady Sarah (Kidman) runs to reunite with Nullah (Walters).

OPPOSITE RIGHT: Nullah (Walters) and Lady Sarah (Kidman) hold each other.

Luhrmann captures the explosive scale of the attack and the emotional ramifications with intense focus. The peaceful, natural landscape of the Outback which viewers had become accustomed to is interrupted by the mechanical hum of planes flying overhead and screams echoing through charcoaled buildings.

The attack occurs on the day Lady Sarah and Nullah are supposed to reunite. Nullah is stranded on Mission Island, which is a fictional location but a reference to the forceful removal of Aboriginal children from their families, traditions, and culture to be "civilised" by Christian missionaries. Mission Island is the first place Japanese forces attacked (again, a creative liberty from Luhrmann) and Drover sets out on a deadly rescue mission. After a nail-biting saviour sequence, Luhrmann follows Lady Sarah barrelling through burning fire and evacuation orders to reunite with Drover and Nullah. They run into each other's arms, and David Hirschfelder's emphatic musical score swoops in with a flurry of strings to accompany the uplifting moment.

LEFT: Lady Sarah (Kidman) and Nullah (Walters) walk through the wilderness.

BELOW: King George (David Gulpilil) and Nullah (Walters).

OPPOSITE: Jackman, Kidman, Walters, Gulpilil and Luhrmann at a press interview.

As well as the historical grounding of the Darwin bombings, Luhrmann's film is underpinned by the themes of national heritage and identity. *Australia* unravels through the eyes of Nullah, whose voiceover brings narrative importance to the representation of Aboriginal Australians and exposes the explicit racism he is subjected to – he is labelled "half-caste" and "creamy" as he wrestles with feelings of non-belonging.

In portraying Aboriginal Australians, *Australia* engages with the fact that the nation's past persists in contemporary issues – like the "stolen generation" child removal policy that Luhrmann unpacks in a text

epilogue. Luhrmann has described this film as his myth of Australia – his connection with the "real" fluctuates between factual and mythologised. Similarly, *Australia*'s representation of marginalised Aboriginal Australians straddles redemption and imagination. Though untouched aspects of Aboriginal belief and life, including the walkabout (Nullah leaves with King George for a nomadic experience) are prominent, Luhrmann does fall back on some cliché stereotypes – like King George's supernatural presence, which is rendered "magical" – in his story.

Nullah's coming-of-age journey with his indigenous identity underscores *Australia*. While many of Luhrmann's characters are granted their hero scene late into the film, Nullah proves his bravery earlier. The Carney men spook Faraway Downs' cattle and cause a stampede towards the edge of a cliff. Nullah races on horseback to block the charging livestock. Facing the horned creatures head-on, he raises his hand and begins to sing under his breath, channelling what he has learnt from King George. Luhrmann cuts quickly between a close-up of Nullah's deep brown gaze and the cows' wild eyes as they grind to a halt, implying a powerful connection between Nullah and nature. This scene shows the young boy has reclaimed the power of his identity – as Drover puts it: "The only thing you really own is your story."

Luhrmann's Outback

On home soil, Luhrmann's epic drama captures the landscapes of Australia with wonder. This rural romance swoons over the landscapes as much as Lady Sarah and Drover's infatuation. As the pair roam across endless miles of land, driving cattle, cinematographer Mandy Walker highlights the sun-blistered Outback's unforgiving nature.

Luhrmann's signature style of visual opulence inflates with Walker's long shots of dusty scorched plains, incredible sunsets and formidable mountainous ravines. As Walker sweeps over various terrains, the aerial shots are borderline panoramic. The cinematography borrows from the classic American western – capturing cattle drives like Howard Hawks' *Red River* – with grand stories relocated to the expansive Outback. Further bolstering *Australia*, unlike Jill Bilcock's hyperactive editing, Dody Dorn and Michael McCusker take a more restrained approach. The Outback lingers on the screen so viewers can properly absorb its grandeur.

Light is a central component of Luhrmann's storytelling. Walker's wide frames find each character under the blinding Australian sun, but the exposing quality of light and the noticeable absence of it imbues *Australia*'s frames with a fantastical quality. Filming in Kununurra, a remote region of northern Western Australia, temperatures soared to a gruelling 43°C and the intensity of sunlight blankets the cattle driving scenes. The sun is a guiding light but a punishing force in the treacherous and vast Never Never desert which the herders traverse.

Luhrmann's lens appreciates Australia's landscapes, whether observing King George atop a mountain or Lady Sarah trudging through the sands. The film syphons through several characters and their differentiating outlooks as Luhrmann examines the beauty of the dusty red plains while contemplating the harsh reality of the country's history.

TOP: Drover (Jackman) in the Outback.

MIDDLE: Lady Sarah (Kidman) and Drover (Jackman) in the Outback.

BOTTOM: Lady Sarah (Kidman) in the Outback.

THE GREAT GATSBY

Literary Adaptation

F. Scott Fitzgerald's novel, *The Great Gatsby*, a classic tale of love, wealth and decadence, makes for illustrious adaptation material for Luhrmann's fifth feature. The Prohibition-era melodrama fuses period music and modern pop in Luhrmann's high-powered portrait of the extravagant Jazz Age. The director was drawn to Fitzgerald's twenties-era narrative for its engrossing complexity, and endeavoured to bring New York City's zeitgeist to modern audiences with the same titillating excitement which 1920s readers were seized by.

The Great Gatsby sees Luhrmannisms on full display. The director drops viewers right in the middle of this story, set in the summer of 1922 – a barrage of intense imagery presents a montage of New York City's hysteria with eye-popping visuals as stocks climb, businessmen party and champagne flutes overflow. Luhrmann's elaborating, enticing stylings are, as always, immediately confronting in this doomed tale of money, love and the American Dream.

LEFT: *The Great Gatsby* movie poster.

RIGHT: The dramatic reveal of Gatsby (Leonardo DiCaprio).

The eponymous James Gatz (DiCaprio), known as Jay Gatsby, is a suave millionaire and man of mystery famed for throwing bombastic parties every weekend. If you listen to the rumours, Gatsby is a German spy, the Kaiser's assassin, "richer than God", a prince, and he does not exist. Naturally, aspiring writer Nick Carraway (Tobey Maguire) is intrigued to uncover the real Gatsby. The Yale-educated midwesterner is *The Great Gatsby*'s unreliable narrator. The memoir-confession of his time with Gatsby, which he pens from a sanatorium, is the basis for Luhrmann's film.

Like Nick, viewers are initially granted glimpses of Gatsby as a distant figure standing in a window and as a silhouetted figure on the end of his dock, reaching towards the pulsing green light from the house across the harbour. The real reveal of Gatsby is an ostentatious moment, even for this director. Gatsby hands Nick a drink, masquerading as a waiter, before turning on the balcony just as fireworks erupt. He coolly raises a champagne glass in a toast with a charismatic smile and sparkling eyes. It's an opulent display of theatrics where Luhrmann makes it crystal clear that Gatsby is the conductor of this orchestra.

OPPOSITE: Nick (Maguire) and Gatsby (DiCaprio).

LEFT: Gatsby (DiCaprio) peering out of his window.

BELOW: Gatsby (DiCaprio) raises his glass.

Though surrounded by wealth and privilege, Gatsby is after something money cannot buy. Five years ago, Gatsby courted Southern belle Daisy (Carey Mulligan), Nick's cousin, but lost her to her philistine husband, Tom Buchanan (Joel Edgerton), when he joined the army. Gatsby is now obsessed with recapturing Daisy, who lives across the harbour from him, and plans to reignite their dormant romance.

ABOVE: Luhrmann directing DiCaprio and Mulligan on the set of *The Great Gatsby*.

Luhrmann's film marked the fifth notable adaptation of *The Great Gatsby*. Departing from its predecessors, Luhrmann and co-writer Craig Pearce made noticeable changes to Fitzgerald's plot. Though Luhrmann lifted some direct dialogue from the page for the screen, he did take creative liberties that some critics felt betrayed Fitzgerald's novel. For instance, Nick's sentimental narration lures Fitzgerald's narrative into Luhrmann's histrionic realm.

ABOVE: Luhrmann directing on the set of *The Great Gatsby*.

The Myth of Man

In *The Great Gatsby*, Luhrmann reunites with DiCaprio. 17 years on from Romeo, DiCaprio's once cherubic face has handsomely matured. With Gatsby, DiCaprio has a blank canvas to spill troubled masculinity, hopeless romanticism and tranquil fantasy.

While Luhrmann creates a world of artifice Gatsby is doing the same; he generates an illusion conjured through body, voice and history. Gatsby has layers to him – he's playing the man he wants to be, the businessman others need him to be, the lover he hopes to be and the friend he wishes he had. Through the eyes of Nick, Gatsby's theatrical layers are peeled away to reveal a man with an incompatible dream of love. His edited tales of being at war and dominating the stock market seem impressive, but Gatsby is from humble beginnings. He

was born poor and worked his way up to the top, but tug at one of his golden fraying threads and his entire life threatens to unravel. Yet he still plays the part and dons dapper suits, including a salmon pink-striped suit, that paint him as an elegant member of high society.

OPPOSITE: Luhrmann on set with DiCaprio.

TOP: Gatsby (DiCaprio) at one of his parties.

BOTTOM: A younger Gatsby (DiCaprio) goes to war and leaves Daisy (Mulligan) behind.

Alongside DiCaprio's nuanced performance is the editing of Matt Villa, Jason Ballantine and Jonathan Redmond that bolsters Gatsby's self-invented mysticism. Smartly timed transition cuts imply that Gatsby is clairvoyant, knowing everything about everyone – their thoughts and feelings. He predicts encounters, worms his way into Nick's life to get closer to Daisy and anticipates phone calls. Nick recognises this side of Gatsby, comparing the man's sensitive surveillance to "one of those intricate machines that register earthquakes ten thousand miles away".

One integral scene is Gatsby's long-awaited reunion with Daisy. Gatsby arrives at Nick's home in a sharp all-white suit, a flurry of his staff in tow with excessive flower bouquets and tall cakes to impress his former lover. Because Luhrmann embeds viewers in Gatsby's momentous parties, the film's quieter moments are starkly intimate. When Daisy arrives, Gatsby goes from a charismatic man to a nervous boy: she is his weakness.

When Daisy enters, Gatsby flees outside into the rain and re-enters through the front door. He pushes back his sopping wet hair, the dishevelled exterior now matching the frazzled interior. Luhrmann draws closer to each one of them, holding centrally framed close-ups. With her sleek blonde bob and elegant lace dress, Daisy is shocked to see the man, but there's an undeniable, unspoken connection. They take their tea the same way and sip simultaneously. As they reconnect, the rain stops and the sun comes out, mirroring the illumination of their rekindled desire.

Furthermore, the pulsing green light at the end of the Buchanans' dock embodies Gatsby's longing for Daisy. The luminescence becomes symbolic in *The Great Gatsby* as if Gatsby's pure desire for Daisy fuels its brightness.

OPPOSITE: Gatsby (DiCaprio) seems frustrated on the phone.

TOP: Gatsby (Luhrmann) sits waiting for Daisy (Mulligan).

MIDDLE: Daisy (Mulligan) arrives at Nick's (Maguire) flower-covered home.

BOTTOM: Daisy (Mulligan) and Gatsby (DiCaprio) are reunited.

The Roaring Twenties

The Roaring Twenties, a period of rapid economic growth and social change, is the perfect setting for Luhrmann to invest in heightened, superfluous glamour for his sybaritic extravaganza. Luhrmann's poetic fancy is divided between the old money of East Egg, Gatsby's West Egg riches, and the wasteland of Valley of Ashes that lies in between. It is Gatsby's mansion where Luhrmannisms are dialled up to the max, with weekend parties that showcase the seductive nature of riches. Cinematographer Simon Duggan's camera swoops through the kaleidoscopic parties that Nick likens to "an amusement park".

Dramatic organ music accompanies Nick gawking at the ridiculous lavishness of Gatsby's home: roulette tables, swimming pools, floor-to-ceiling libraries and ballrooms galore. There is a self-aware superficiality to these sets that reflect the style of 1920s Hollywood Regency, characterised by gilded accents, velvet fabrics, mirrored furniture and sparkly chandeliers. However, the high-gloss sumptuousness of interior design appears desperately lonely when Gatsby wanders the expansive halls alone.

OPPOSITE:
Gatsby's (DiCaprio) impressive mansion.

TOP: Gatsby (DiCaprio) lounging in his lavish home.

BOTTOM: Gatsby's (DiCaprio) fancy parties.

Gatsby's guests flock to his parties in a flurry of diamonds and sequins. Their eye-catching exteriors allow a projection of one's ideal self. The costume designer, once again Catherine Martin, altered pieces from the Prada and Miu Miu fashion archives to elevate 1920s-inspired looks for a modern audience with European flair and highly sophisticated elegance. Instead of pushing for historical accuracy, Martin worked off 1920s silhouettes to create nostalgia for the ultra-luxe flapper style. It is easy to get swept up in the excess,

ABOVE: Gatsby's (DiCaprio) party is in full swing.

OPPOSITE: Daisy (Mulligan) lounging in an elegant dress.

but Luhrmann is careful to present this fantasy as, quite simply, a fantasy. The surface superficiality of Gatsby's weekend parties is all a ploy to reunite with Daisy. He is hopeful his love will transcend time and place in what is a fantastical assertion. Gatsby is the ultimate dreamer; it flows in his blood, but *The Great Gatsby* ultimately finds and exposes the cracks in this dreamy facade. For all its gorgeous opulence, Luhrmann's film lands as a cautionary tale about self-delusion.

A Weekend at Gatsby's

The illicit but fated romance between Gatsby and Daisy prompts emotional swells in Luhrmann's plot. After the pair reunite, a montage-like arrangement sees them living out their perfect fantasy, frolicking under the glowing sunshine.

The lovers then admit their feelings scored to Lana Del Rey's haunting 'Young and Beautiful'. The film's soundtrack is a heady fusion of contemporary hip-hop with 20th-century jazz. In this sequence, the arresting lyricism about being apprehensive towards love comes from the perspective of Daisy. As in *Romeo + Juliet* and *Moulin Rouge!*, Luhrmann does not utilise music as a backdrop but as a direct articulation of internal thought. Del Rey's song seems to take the words right out of Daisy and Gatsby's mouths.

LEFT: Gatsby (DiCaprio) and Daisy (Mulligan).

OPPOSITE TOP: Gatsby (DiCaprio), Daisy (Mulligan), and Tom (Edgerton) descend to the dance floor.

OPPOSITE BOTTOM: Nick (Maguire), Gatsby (DiCaprio), Daisy (Mulligan) and Tom (Joel Edgerton) at Gatsby's party.

When Daisy finally attends one of Gatsby's opulent weekend parties, she arrives with her husband. Throughout the night, Luhrmann repeatedly frames Daisy's lover and husband on either side of her. Though it's Tom's arm she holds onto upon arrival, it's Gatsby's hand she takes on the dance floor. Also, Luhrmann implements the framing device when these characters take a seat – Luhrmann's camera is placed at Daisy's eye level, admiring her sparkly headband and pearl bracelet. In the background, slightly out of focus, Tom and Gatsby are framed as if perched on her shoulders. They appear like a devil and an angel looming over her body. The confrontational shot heightens the rivalry that is escalating.

Later, this shot is transposed for the topic of Daisy's infidelity. In the sweltering heat of a Plaza Hotel suite, Gatsby pleads for Daisy to reveal to her husband that she never loved him. Luhrmann bounces between a close-up of the disbelieving Tom while Gatsby and Daisy share the frame. As Gatsby keeps begging Daisy to confess, Luhrmann finds Tom centred in the background of their two-shot as if he is driving a physical wedge between the pair. It is a reversed mirror of the shot where Daisy is centred: a position of power where Daisy can choose between the men. When this shot applies to Tom, it reinforces his refusal of Daisy's freedom and knowledge of Gatsby's lies that keep the lovers apart.

To this point in the scene, cinematographer Duggan's frames are fixed shots. That all changes when Tom reveals Gatsby's illegal dealings and self-conducted illusions. Luhrmann's camera hastily swaps between four different angles of Gatsby grabbing Tom and raising his fist, a suddenly dynamic scene that spikes the film's pacing. A red-faced Gatsby menacingly stands over Tom, screaming from a Dutch angle – the tilted disorientation emphasises the uncharacteristic nature of this hysterical outburst. In seconds, Gatsby's face soothes as he realises he has shown his cards and revealed a version of himself that he had been trying so hard to conceal. He stands up, pushes his hair back into place and re-buttons his suit jacket. But it's too late. Gatsby has sealed his fate and lost his biggest dream: Daisy.

OPPOSITE: Tom (Edgerton) stands between Daisy (Mulligan) and Gatsby (DiCaprio).

ABOVE: Gatsby (DiCaprio) is about to throw a punch.

Under the Eyes of God

Stood in the Valley of Ashes, a billboard of Dr T.J. Eckleburg's blue eyes watch over disasters with an omnipresence. The eyes seem to stare towards the apex of Gatsby's end, his assassination – which plays out in Luhrmann's film, unlike Fitzgerald's text – enthrallingly foreshadowed. On the ill-fated trip to the Plaza Hotel, Gatsby drives Daisy while Tom chauffeurs Jordan (Elizabeth Debicki) and Nick. The latter peels off the road to fill up with fuel at George Wilson's (Jason Clarke) garage – the man whose wife, Myrtle (Isla Fisher), Tom is having an affair with. In a cruel twist of fate, if he had not stopped, Myrtle would not have seen Tom driving Gatsby's car, a vehicle that would later kill her. There, with an omnibenevolent gaze, Dr T.J. Eckleburg's disembodied eyes stare into Nick's soul to warn him of the forthcoming disaster.

When the group returns, Gatsby and Tom have now swapped cars. Myrtle runs in front of Gatsby's car, mistaking the driver for Tom. She is struck and instantly killed. Dr T.J. Eckleburg's persistent stare watches over the chaos as if it's been expecting such catastrophe. Those blue eyes of tragedy are even present as Gatsby meets his end.

After the death of his wife, George sets off on a revenge rampage, and Tom directs his anger towards Gatsby, framing him as Myrtle's lover and killer. Unaware, Gatsby is taking his last swim of the summer. His phone rings – expecting it to be Daisy declaring her love. When Gatsby begins to climb the pool ladder, his crystal azure eyes are strikingly familiar.

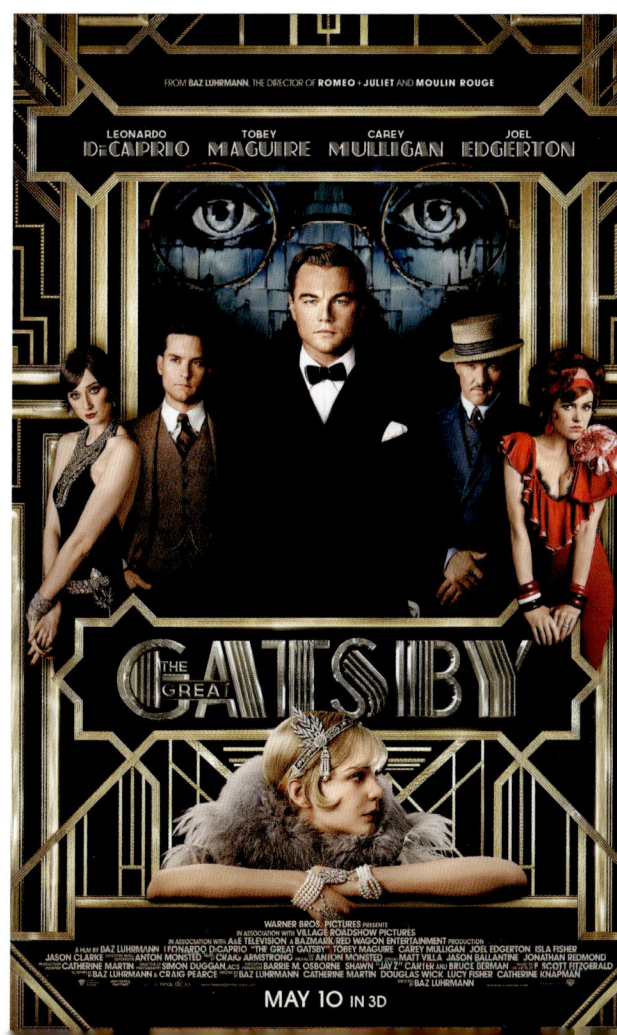

OPPOSITE LEFT: Nick (Maguire), Jordan (Debicki), and Tom (Edgerton) driving.

OPPOSITE RIGHT: Tom (Edgerton) at George (Clarke) and Myrtle's (Fisher) garage.

RIGHT: Dr T.J. Eckleburg's eyes in the background of *The Great Gatsby* poster.

Blue eyes project admonishment, but this time, it is not Dr T.J. Eckleburg's gaze on Nick, but Gatsby's eyes staring at the viewer. He is just about to leave the pool when George pulls the trigger. Gatsby's face breaks into shocked anguish as he realises his dreams are over; Luhrmann's film falls into a rare silence before Gatsby falls backwards into the pool with a loud splash.

Luhrmann's camera whizzes across the harbour to Daisy's house in time with Gatsby's last inhale. As he releases a wounded exhale, the camera boomerangs back. As Nick puts it: "His dream must have seemed so close that he could hardly fail to grasp it. He did not know that it was already behind him." Luhrmann's tragedy ends with Gatsby's death as he believed he was so close to winning Daisy's heart. The heartbreak is as cataclysmic as Satine's curtain call or Romeo and Juliet's end in the Capulet tomb.

It was not Daisy calling for Gatsby, but Nick. For him, the sound of a bullet down the phone marks the death of the American Dream. Luhrmann implies it, too – if Gatsby could not achieve his dream

surrounded by the vast carelessness of the rich, what hope do the rest of us have? As Luhrmann's film concludes, the pulsing green light on the Buchanans' dock reappears. In Gatsby's last moment, he believes Daisy is within reaching distance, but the glowing beacon that held his hopes gets lost amidst the mist.

It is clear the love that Gatsby fostered for Daisy could never be realised, despite the elaborately constructed persona he devised for her. There is a double-lensed romanticism to the film: not only is Gatsby's version of Daisy conjured after years of fantasising, but there is also the version of Gatsby that Nick nostalgically portrays. Though this narrator revisits his memories of Gatsby, Luhrmann leaves it up to us to ponder who exactly is the *real* Gatsby: a financial crook, a great man, or a myth that proliferated beyond expectation. We get to decide.

OPPOSITE TOP: Gatsby (DiCaprio) rises from his swimming pool.

OPPOSITE BOTTOM: Nick (Maguire) makes his last phone call to Gatsby (DiCaprio).

RIGHT: Gatsby (DiCaprio) and Daisy (Mulligan) dance.

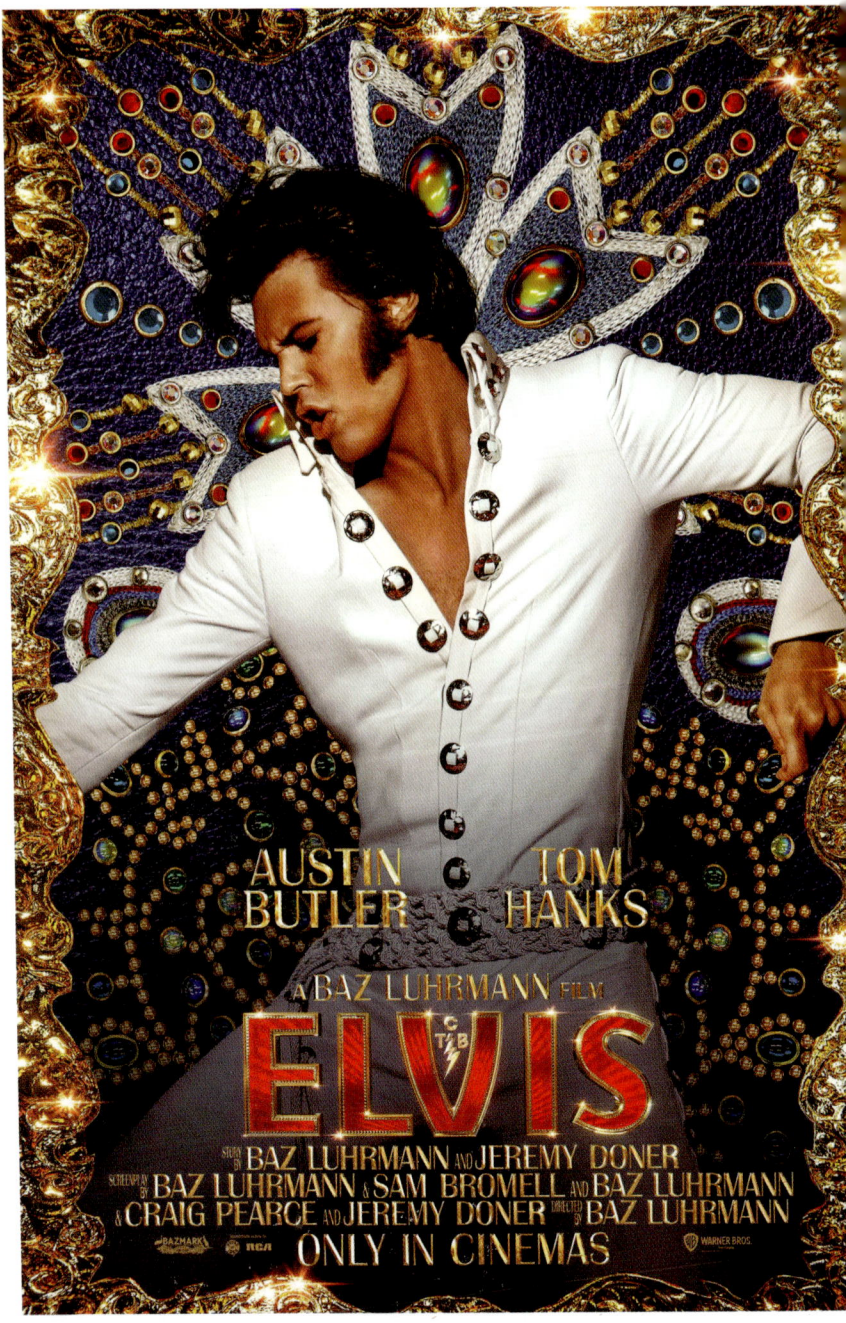

ELVIS

LEFT: The *Elvis* movie poster.

BELOW: Luhrmann and Butler posing on the red carpet.

The King of Rock 'n' Roll

With Elvis Presley, Luhrmann finds his ultimate match in showmanship. The director revives the King of Rock 'n' Roll for this grand jukebox biopic to chronicle the pinnacle of his fame, when the mythic musician became a symbolic cypher of innovation instead of skin and bones. For Luhrmann, Elvis was an object of childhood fascination sparked by the singer's stint in Hollywood. However, in watching the timeless icon's life play out, Luhrmann has remarked that he came to understand Elvis's life as a sort of Shakespearean tragedy. With *Elvis*, Luhrmann asks what the star means to an audience today by retracing the sonic legend's steps to becoming a worldwide phenomenon.

Bringing the King of Rock 'n' Roll back to life is no easy task, but Luhrmann struck gold with Austin Butler. The actor submerged himself in the world of Graceland, extensively studying everything and anything Elvis-related. Butler's portrayal is not an imitation

but an uncanny emulation of Elvis's vocal timbre and rhythmic movement. Butler executes this so well that pre-1960s scenes feature Butler's voice overlaying recordings of the real-life Elvis – the blend between the two is seamless. Casting a little-known actor for Elvis was a calculated move from Luhrmann, ensuring a clean slate for his portrait of the singer void of previous character associations.

Luhmann kicks off with a classic Luhrmannism: beginning at the end. The introduction of Elvis's former manager, Colonel Tom Parker (Tom Hanks), sees him dying. "I didn't kill him. I made Elvis Presley," Tom croaks from a hospital bed, his IV drip framing the skyline. Tom's unreliable voiceover steers this narrative, refuting claims of his insidious nature and pleading a case of innocence. While Elvis was the showman, Tom was the snowman, a Gatsby-esque character who feeds on the success of his stars. Tom is a "mister nobody from nowhere" who seemingly materialised in pursuit of the American Dream; his name is not even Tom Parker, and he is not a Colonel. "We are the same, you and I: two odd, lonely children reaching for eternity," Tom tells Elvis, luring him into a gilded cage.

It is in a carnival house of mirrors where Tom poaches Elvis. The carnival is a perfect setting for this interaction – the circus is the American entertainment industry, a parade of flashing lights, bold colours and big smiles that is all for show – and Tom is the ringmaster of this circus. "You look lost," Tom tells a young Elvis whose refracted reflection surrounds them. Tom easily manipulates Elvis, seeing him lost in both the mirror maze and his budding career.

The pair then get on a Ferris Wheel, where Tom proposes that Elvis becomes another act in his carnival. As the Ferris Wheel lurches into action, they strike a deal while admiring the twinkling circus lights they fly above. With the hesitant blessing of his mother, Gladys (Helen Thomson), and father, Vernon (Richard Roxburgh, who plays the Duke in *Moulin Rouge!*), Elvis signs on the dotted line. With the deal, the Presley family rose from poverty and bought Elvis's dream pink Cadillac and the residence of Graceland, their home.

OPPOSITE: Butler as Elvis.

TOP: Tom (Hanks) and Elvis (Butler) on a carnival Ferris Wheel.

LEFT: Elvis (Butler), Gladys (Thomson), Tom (Hanks), and Vernon (Roxburgh) sign Elvis's contract.

Remodelling the Biopic

Luhrmann's *Elvis* is not a conventional biopic. As with all of his films, Luhrmann's signature decorative style and distinctly anti-nostalgic approach are branded all over *Elvis*. The film marks a culmination of Luhrmann's filmography. The kaleidoscopic biopic embodies the artistic dreams of *Strictly Ballroom*, the extravagance of *Romeo + Juliet*, the turbo-charged musical melodies of *Moulin Rouge!*, the extensive ambition of *Australia* and the irreverent personalities of *The Great Gatsby*.

ABOVE: Luhrmann, DeJonge, and Butler on set.

OPPOSITE LEFT: Elvis (Butler) and Priscilla (DeJonge).

OPPOSITE RIGHT: Luhrmann and Butler on set.

Luhrmann situates the details of Elvis's life – his deployment in the army, his relationship, marriage and divorce with Priscilla (Olivia DeJonge), his stint as an actor in Hollywood cinema and the death of his mother – within the framework of his music career. Luhrmann jumps from performance to performance, each coinciding with chapters in the legend's life. Ultimately, the stage becomes Elvis's space for releasing pent-up emotion that ranges from fiercely frustrated to painfully heartbroken.

The lavish film follows hot on the heels of the recent releases of Hollywood music star biopics *Bohemian Rhapsody* (2018) and *Rocketman* (2019), which respectively charted the lives of music icons Freddie Mercury and Elton John. However, in charting details from an unorthodox childhood in Memphis to his untimely death, Luhrmann's recounting of Elvis's life differentiates from the film's genre counterparts with its storyteller. With Tom being the puppetmaster and Elvis the puppet, Luhrmann uses Tom's narration to highlight the good and bad of Elvis's career within the cultural context of the 1950s, 1960s and 1970s. In busying the chronological biopic narrative, Luhrmann departs from the typical genre template.

Elvis on the Mic

Elvis's performances are set pieces that amp up volume and vibrancy which makes them perfect for Luhrmannisms. Elvis nervously steps on stage with "greasy hair, girly make-up", and a soft pink suit that enhances his dreamy aura for his first show. The opening notes of 'Baby, Let's Play House' begin, and Elvis's body begins to vibrate under the glare of a single spotlight.

Elvis's smouldering movements seem powered by the increasingly feral screams of carnal desire from the crowd. His gyrating hips prompt the first spark of intense sex appeal, and even Tom cannot rip his eyes away from his star power. This heady atmosphere informs cinematographer Mandy Walker's frenzied frames as breakneck whip pans, energetic zooms and increasingly brisk editing cuts capture Elvis's thrusting crotch and the audience's possessed shrieks. The kinetic sweeping camera seems to dance with Elvis on stage as Tom proudly declares him "the greatest carnival attraction I'd ever seen".

OPPOSITE: Elvis (Butler) graces the stage.

LEFT: Elvis (Butler) performs at the Louisiana Hayride.

BELOW: Elvis (Butler) performs to a screaming crowd.

This first performance showcases that a star has been born and contextualises Elvis's love for music. A flashback to a young Elvis (Chaydon Jay) sees him hear the blues wail of Arthur "Big Boy" Crudup's (Gary Clark Jr.) 'That's All Right Mama', a song Elvis went on to cover. The young Elvis approaches a Black revival service in a tent that billows with the power of the worshipers' gospel melodies. Crudup's high-pitched vocals meld with Elvis's present-day low hums as the young Elvis is drawn into the centre of the crowd, arms raised and eyes closed, as music bewitches his body. Cutting from this sequence to Elvis gracing the stage, Luhrmann draws a parallel between the raised hands of worshippers and Elvis's frantic fans. Luhrmann frames these two moments as monumental; in the first, Elvis experiences what it is like to be taken over by music, and then he realises he is in possession of the power to enchant an audience with music.

The stage also becomes a pedestal for rebellion. With mounting magnetism, Elvis became a target of conservative moral panic for his power to corrupt the minds of white youth with his "hips of a Black man". Despite threats of imprisonment, Elvis brushes off the family-friendly Elvis that Tom had prepared for him. Luhrmann follows Elvis from behind as he marches onto the Russwood Park stage in 1956, his silhouette outlined by the insistent flash of paparazzi cameras. When the camera rounds Elvis, Luhrmann reveals the performer's face in a close-up that accentuates his moody stare through thick eyelashes and smoky eyeshadow.

OPPOSITE: Elvis (Butler) is watching the amusements in a carnival.

ABOVE: Tom (Hanks) warns Elvis (Butler) before he steps on stage.

Tom's once hopeful expression morphs into a panicked circus master as his main act squares up to sing 'Trouble', an aptly named proto-punk rock track. Elvis sings with a growling snarl, telling the audience to look in his direction if they are looking for trouble and that he is no longer abiding by orders. He tells them he is miserable. Rescinding the commercial image, Elvis flouts the police threats as he writhes on the floor screaming, "I'm evil!" What is problematic for authorities is iconic through Luhrmann's lens. The director shoots

Elvis's concert from several angles, on and off stage, but positioning the camera in the audience embeds viewers in the hysteria and gives Luhrmann the chance to replicate the energy of what it would be like to attend the sexually charged, provocative show where Elvis swung his hips with a newfound vigour.

BELOW: Elvis (Butler) with excited fans.

Blues and Gospel

Documenting decades of Elvis's career, Luhrmann's film spans extensive American culture and Elvis's relationship with Black artists. The singer was heavily influenced by Black musicians whose songs he would then cover for mainstream radio play; some regard it as appreciation, and others remark that it is appropriation and outright theft. Luhrmann's portrait explicitly points to the origins of Elvis's music and sets out to pay deference to the original gospel and blues artists who inspired him.

Luhrmann quickly establishes that Elvis's music is rooted in the

exemplariness of Black music – the singer frequently resides at Club Handy, a legendary Memphis club on Beale Street. Here, his personal style and acclaimed sound became informed by Black culture. At Club Handy, Elvis witnesses performances by Little Richard (Alton Mason), Sister Rosetta Tharpe (Yola), and Big Mama Thornton (Shonka Dukureh). Luhrmann makes it abundantly clear: without Black culture, we would have no Elvis Presley.

BELOW LEFT: Elvis (Butler) arrives at Club Handy.

BELOW RIGHT: Little Richard (Mason) performs at Club Handy.

LEFT: Elvis (Butler) and B.B. King (Harrison Jr) at Club Handy.

OPPOSITE: Big Mama Thornton (Dukureh) performing at Club Handy.

Elvis does explore the sentiment that the star's whiteness enabled him to get famous by covering songs from Black origins – like Crudup's blues classic 'That's All Right Mama' and Thornton's 'Hound Dog'. Luhrmann tracks this process when Elvis and his friend B.B. King (Kelvin Harrison Jr.) are enthralled by Little Richard's 'Tutti Frutti' performance at Club Handy. King confides in Elvis that he believes Elvis could record the track and make considerably more money than Little Richard had, and he does.

Elvis's mainstream success came with a controversial tag: he could stoke racial hostility and corrupt the minds of white youth in a violation of de jure segregation. Luhrmann inserts news broadcasts of Martin Luther King Jr. and Robert F. Kennedy's assassinations in 1968, two events that Luhrmann spotlights as wake-up calls for Elvis. The singer grows increasingly paranoid about being murdered, and with Tom tightening his grip on Elvis's image as a clean-cut all-American without a blemish on his reputation, Elvis's manager silences his support of the civil rights movement.

Luhrmann also knows the power of music on an audience. The *Elvis* soundtrack transcends time and setting with music producer Elliott Wheeler's insertion of contemporary flourishes. This includes Doja Cat's 'Vegas' that samples Big Mama Thornton's 'Hound Dog' (which Elvis went on to cover) and Swae Lee and Diplo's 'Tupelo Shuffle' (which samples Elvis's cover of 'That's All Right' that plays as a young Elvis sees Crudup's original performance) alongside the blend of country, blues, and gospel that infuses the film score.

Las Vegas Tragedy

The final act of *Elvis* comes to rest in Las Vegas, beneath the bright lights and surrounding ring of slot machines. It is here that Luhrmann unravels Elvis's Las Vegas residency, looking beyond the rhinestone-encrusted glitz to find a star running out of fuel to burn. Elvis reaches the apex of his career, but his life shatters in his hands: Priscilla leaves him and takes their child with her, while Elvis drifts from his once exuberant stardom.

Elvis's five-year residence at Vegas's International Hotel begins with him performing in the now-famous white-flared jumpsuit while Tom conducts business in the crowd. He's sat with the Hotel's businessmen as they draw out a deal worth millions on the tablecloth

that would lock Elvis into performance exclusivity and wipe Tom's mountain of debt. It's no coincidence that Luhrmann times this interaction as Elvis sings 'Suspicious Minds' and tells his audience he is caught in a trap he can't free himself from. Elvis goes wild on stage like a trapped animal, as Tom agrees to the clause "as long as that boy stays on that stage".

Elvis's US tour, with all the triumphant ups and heartbreaking downs, is summarised in a frantic montage to 'Burning Love' as the years fly by and Elvis's life descends into injection needles, rattling pill bottles and sneaking women into hotels. These moments are framed by a hazy vignette as if the world is going in and out of focus as Elvis exists in a perpetual drug-induced state. Luhrmann's film now almost exclusively positions Elvis on stage – it's here where he thrives but also where he crumbles. Luhrmann's climactic moment comes with Elvis turning on Tom during a Vegas show. "I can't get out, 'cus Colonel's got some big debts, baby," he slurs. Cinematographer Walker captures the singer sweating and clutching his head in a spinning dutch angle shot from above. The awkward camera position accompanies the unusual feat of an Elvis show falling into silence.

OPPOSITE TOP: Elvis (Butler) arrives in Las Vegas.

OPPOSITE BOTTOM: Elvis (Butler) at his Las Vegas residency.

TOP: Tom (Hanks) and Elvis (Butler) plan a show.

RIGHT: Elvis (Butler) collapses backstage before a show.

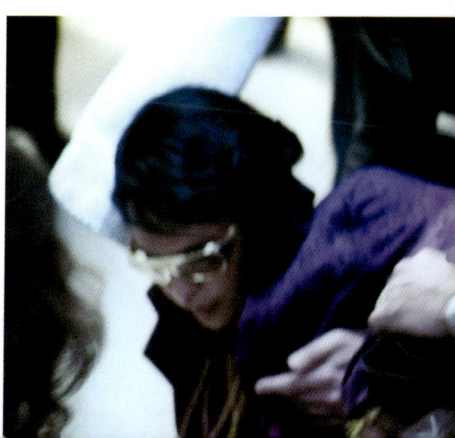

Elvis can stretch his wings, but he cannot fly far. Tom has ensured Elvis cannot survive without him, so their symbiotic, parasitic relationship continues. Tom's recollection of Elvis's career concludes with a show on 21st June, 1977, in Rapid City, South Dakota, with his 'Unchained Melody' performance. He's unable to stand, and his speech is indistinct, but his voice rings out with pure heart and soul. Luhrmann's final shot of his Elvis is a slow zoom, drawing closer to a headshot frame of the King of Rock 'n' Roll.

Luhrmann then hard cuts to a practically identical shot of the real Elvis singing 'Unchained Melody'. The transition from Butler to Presley is a gut punch that reinforces the legitimacy of *Elvis*. Luhrmann uses the archival material to clarify his film's relationship between fiction and reality. Concert footage alternating between home videos of Elvis, Priscilla and their child shows Luhrmann's theatrical retelling is somewhat truthful but exists at an arm's length from the real man. Luhrmann's conclusion ultimately hands his film back to the real star, giving Elvis the last word.

OPPOSITE: Elvis (Butler) and adoring fans.

ABOVE: Elvis (Butler) playing the piano.

THE CURTAIN FALLS...

Heartbreakingly Beautiful Endings

As the band fades out and the curtain comes down, Luhrmann's films invariably conclude with devastating heartbreak. Though Luhrmann reveals the ending in his films at the beginning (as per the Red Curtain Trilogy), after being lost in the illustrious cinematic worlds the tragedies still sneak up on the audience.

The Australian auteur may be a polarising director because of his commitment to a heightened reality and lack of subtext. Nevertheless, his signature style is singular. Luhrmann approaches his films as if he is welcoming viewers into a story. The emotional and moral stories transport audience members into fabulous worlds where anything seems possible. However, in the final act, the delusion is shattered as Luhrmann rips away character dreams for a powerfully heartbreaking curtain call. The power of loss ripples through the director's filmography, and these agonisingly tragic endings leave Luhrmann's stories lingering at the forefront of viewers' minds.

OPPOSITE TOP: Satine (Kidman) and Christian (McGregor) duet in *Moulin Rouge!*.

OPPOSITE BOTTOM: Gatsby's (DiCaprio) extravagant parties in *The Great Gatsby*.

In Another World

The wacky worlds created by Luhrmann become an escapist reality. The theatrical stories bridge film and theatre in their conception, but many of the contemporary auteur's productions have also gone on to exist beyond the silver screen.

Luhrmann's debut, *Strictly Ballroom*, originated on stage before the screen. But a new stage musical of *Strictly Ballroom* adapted the film's plot, revisiting the original story's roots. The stage musical premiered in 2014 at a Sydney theatre before moving to Melbourne and Brisbane. A further revised production had its British premiere in 2016 and North America in 2017.

The glitz, glory and grandeur of *Moulin Rouge!* also has had a second life on stage. The Piccadilly Theatre in London's West End is the home of a new incarnation of the bohemian and courtesan's love story. Bringing *Moulin Rouge!*'s hyperactive spectacle to the stage, where the film's drama unfolds, is like a homecoming for Luhrmann's glittering story.

Australia, Luhrmann's expansive portrait of his home country, has also been uniquely extended beyond its cinematic identity. When sorting

through the original film of his 2008 wartime epic, Luhrmann decided to serialise *Australia* into a six-part series, *Faraway Downs*, released in 2023. The show relies on much of the nearly three-hour-long film's material but is expanded with a re-edited story, previously deleted scenes and a new score.

OPPOSITE: Scott (Jonny Labey) and Fran (Zizi Strallen) in *Strictly Ballroom the Musical*.

TOP: The West End production of *Moulin Rouge! The Musical*.

ABOVE: The *Faraway Downs* promotional poster.

Luhrmann's Cinema

Luhrmann is a showman who invites viewers into his intoxicating cinematic spectacles that are so compelling you'll never want them to end. To date, Luhrmann's six features have maintained an untampered flamboyance as he identifies beauty in even the darkest turns of his films.

Renowned for his Red Curtain Trilogy, from which Luhrmannisms were born, the director's signature style of lingering close-ups, slow-motion action shots, agitated editing, and marvellous production design is so distinctive that his filmmaking can be regarded loosely as its own genre. *Strictly Ballroom*, *Romeo + Juliet* and *Moulin Rouge!* sparkle with emotional poeticism while *Australia* is epic in proportion, *The Great Gatsby* is a mystical feat, and *Elvis* features iconic personalities.

Outrageous characters and far-fetched plots are given verisimilitude in Luhrmann's hallmark fantasies. The director unabashedly embraces the artificiality of cinema; in his universes, we dance amongst the stars while being serenaded by the moon. So much so, if we understand cinema as the suspension of disbelief as the limits of reality dissolve, then Luhrmann's films can be regarded as the epitome of cinematic art.

OPPOSITE: Luhrmann on the set of *Elvis*.

ABOVE: Luhrmann on the set of *The Great Gatsby*.

Image Credits

(t) = top, (m) = middle, (b) = bottom, (c) = centre, (l) = left, (r) = right

Page 7 AJ Pics/Alamy; 8 (t) Entertainment Pictures/Alamy; 8 (b) Moviestore Collection Ltd; 9 Photo 12/Alamy; 10 Cinematic/Alamy; 11 (t) LANDMARK MEDIA/Alamy; 11 (b) Everett Collection Inc/Alamy; 12 Cinematic/Alamy; 13 Album/Alamy; 14 Allstar Picture Library Ltd/Alamy; 15 Barry King/Getty; 16 AJ Pics/Alamy; 17 (t) LANDMARK MEDIA/Alamy; 17 (b) Pictorial Press Ltd/Alamy; 18 Moviestore Collection Ltd/Alamy; 19 Barry King/Getty; 20 Moviestore Collection Ltd/Alamy; 21 (t) Maximum Film/Alamy; 21 (b) Cinematic/Alamy; 22 Cinematic/Alamy; 23 Cinematic/Alamy; 24-25 Photo 12/Alamy; 27 Entertainment Pictures/Alamy; 28 Entertainment Pictures/Alamy; 29 Moviestore Collection/Alamy; 30 (t) Maximum Film/Alamy; 30 (b) Cinematic/Alamy; 31 Cinematic/Alamy; 32 Moviestore Collection Ltd/Alamy; 33 (t) and (b) Australian Associated Press/Alamy; 34 Moviestore Collection Ltd/Alamy; 35 Photo 12/Alamy; 36 AJ Pics/Alamy; 38 BFA/Alamy; 40 LANDMARK MEDIA/Alamy; 41 (l) and (r) LANDMARK MEDIA/Alamy; 42 Moviestore Collection Ltd/Alamy; 43 (t) LANDMARK MEDIA/Alamy; 43 (b) Album/Alamy; 44 (t) LANDMARK MEDIA/Alamy; 44 (b) Maximum Film/Alamy; 45 Moviestore Collection Ltd/Alamy; 46 (tl) FlixPix/Alamy; 46 (tr) Pictorial Press Ltd/Alamy; 46 (m) LANDMARK MEDIA/Alamy; 46 (b) AJ Pics/Alamy; 49 (t) (m) and (b) LANDMARK MEDIA/Alamy; 50 LANDMARK MEDIA/Alamy; 51 (t) AJ Pics/Alamy; 52 Maximum Film/Alamy; 53 LANDMARK MEDIA/Alamy; 54 (t) United Archives GmbH/Alamy; 54 (b) LANDMARK MEDIA/Alamy; 55 LANDMARK MEDIA/Alamy; 56 Cinematic/Alamy; 57 (t) Cinematic/Alamy; 57 (b) LANDMARK MEDIA/Alamy; 58 Cinematic/Alamy; 59 Moviestore Collection Ltd/Alamy; 60-61 LANDMARK MEDIA/Alamy; 62 Everett Collection Inc/Alamy; 63 AJ Pics/Alamy; 64 Maximum Film/Alamy; 65 (t) AJ Pics/Alamy; 65 (b) Maximum Film/Alamy; 66 Maximum Film/Alamy; 67 (t) PictureLux/The Hollywood Archive/Alamy; 67 (b) Pictorial Press Ltd/Alamy; 68 Maximum Film/Alamy; 69 Cinematic/Alamy; 70 AJ Pics/Alamy; 71 Maximum Film/Alamy; 72 Moviestore Collection Ltd/Alamy; 73 Moviestore Collection Ltd/Alamy; 74 Entertainment Pictures/Alamy; 75 (tl) and (tr) Entertainment Pictures/Alamy; 75 (b) Moviestore Collection Ltd/Alamy; 76-77 Cinematic/Alamy; 78-79 United Archives

PREVIOUS: Satine (Kidman) and Christian (McGregor) dancing above Paris.

GmbH/Alamy; 80 Maximum Film/Alamy; 82 Cinematic/Alamy; 83 AJ Pics/Alamy; 85 Maximum Film/Alamy; 86-87 Pictorial Press/Alamy; 88 Maximum Film/Alamy; 89 Cinematic/Alamy; 91 Cinematic/Alamy; 92-93 Photo 12/Alamy; 94 Photo 12/Alamy; 95 Historic Collection/Alamy; 96 Photo 12/Alamy; 97 (t) and (m) Cinematic/Alamy; 97 (b) Photo 12/Alamy;98 Photo 12/Alamy; 99 (t) Maximum Film/Alamy; 99 (b) Cinematic/Alamy; 100 Album/Alamy; 101 (t) Moviestore Collection Ltd/Alamy; 101 (b) Photo 12/Alamy; 102 (t) Photo 12/Alamy; 102 (b) Maximum Film/Alamy; 103 Album/Alamy; 104 (t) and (b) Cinematic/Alamy; 105 Associated Press/Alamy; 107 (t) Cinematic/Alamy; 107 (m) and (b) Maximum Film/Alamy; 108 Cinematic/Alamy; 109 PictureLux/The Hollywood Archive/Alamy; 110 Photo 12/Alamy; 111 (t) and (b) LANDMARK MEDIA/Alamy; 112 PictureLux/The Hollywood Archive/Alamy; 113 LANDMARK MEDIA/Alamy; 114 PictureLux/The Hollywood Archive/Alamy; 115 (t) PictureLux/The Hollywood Archive/Alamy; 115 (b) LANDMARK MEDIA/Alamy; 116 Photo 12/Alamy; 117 (t) (m) and (b) Album/Alamy; 118 Album/Alamy; 119 (t) Album/Alamy; 119 (b) LANDMARK MEDIA/Alamy; 120 Moviestore Collection Ltd/Alamy; 121 Cinematic/Alamy; 122 Album/Alamy; 123 (t) and (b) Album/Alamy; 124 Everett Collection Inc/Alamy; 125 LANDMARK MEDIA/Alamy; 126 (l) Album/Alamy; 126 (r) Cinematic/Alamy; 127 AJ Pics/Alamy; 128 (t) LANDMARK MEDIA/Alamy; 128 (b) Photo 12/Alamy; 129 Album/Alamy; 130 FlixPix/Alamy; 131 Jon Kopaloff/Getty; 132 Entertainment Pictures/Alamy; 133 (t) Album/Alamy; 133 (b) Entertainment Pictures/Alamy; 134 Album/Alamy; 135 (l) Entertainment Pictures/Alamy; 135 (r) Everett Collection Inc/Alamy; 136 LANDMARK MEDIA/Alamy; 137 (t) Entertainment Pictures/Alamy; 137 (b) LANDMARK MEDIA/Alamy; 138 BFA/Alamy; 139 Moviestore Collection Ltd/Alamy; 140-141 Entertainment Pictures/Alamy; 142 Album/Alamy; 143 Entertainment Pictures/Alamy; 144 Entertainment Pictures/Alamy; 145 Moviestore Collection Ltd/Alamy; 146 (t) Album/Alamy; 146 (b) LANDMARK MEDIA/Alamy; 147 (t) Entertainment Pictures/Alamy; 147 (b) LANDMARK MEDIA/Alamy; 148 Moviestore Collection Ltd/Alamy; 149 Moviestore Collection Ltd/Alamy; 151 (t) Maximum Film/Alamy; 151 (b) Album/Alamy; 152 David Jensen/Alamy; 153 (t) PA Images/Alamy; 153 (b) Barry King/Alamy; 154 Everett Collection Inc/Alamy; 155 LANDMARK MEDIA/Alamy; 156-157 Pictorial Press Ltd/Alamy